HAUNTED FELLS POINT

GHOSTS OF BALTIMORE'S WATERFRONT

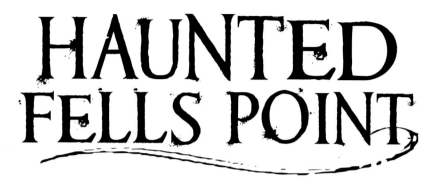

MIKE CARTER AND JULIA DRAY

Haunted America

Published by Haunted America

A Division of The History Press

Charleston, SC

www.historypress.net

First published 2017

Manufactured in the United States

ISBN 9781467136785

Library of Congress Control Number: 2016950701

Notice: The information in this book is true and complete to the best of our knowledge. It is offered without guarantee on the part of the authors or The History Press. The authors and The History Press disclaim all liability in connection with the use of this book.

CONTENTS

AUTHORS' NOTE

People ask me all of the time, "Is Fells Point *really* haunted?" The short answer—"Yes!" Given the overwhelming number of eyewitness accounts from credible witnesses, the city's sordid past, an array of colorful characters and a troubled history filled with murder, untimely deaths and mayhem of all sorts, it's just the kind of place where, if you believe that ghosts are real, they are most likely to be found.

How did we end up making the jump from Annapolis to Baltimore? And why Fells Point? Both Julia and I firmly believed that Fells Point was a perfect locale for our particular brand of historical research and exciting storytelling. It is filled with rogues and scoundrels, pirates and privateers, legend and lore and, of course, lots of hauntings. But the truth is I saw a niche, and I filled it using the successes of the Annapolis Ghost Tours and that of our first book, *Haunted Annapolis: Ghosts of the Capital City*, as a foundation, as well as our unique ability to make both the tumultuous history and eerie hauntings of Fells Point come alive.

It all began when my wife and I were on a visit to Charleston, South Carolina, and Savannah, Georgia, in the summer of 2001, and we went on a ghost tour for the first time in our lives. This was not some preplanned item on our travel itinerary but rather a totally organic experience that completely changed my future. Like many travelers, we were having breakfast at a table in a very busy bagel shop in historic Charleston, on which some previous diner had left a random stack of rack cards. My wife began thumbing through them and, finding several for ghost tours, suggested that it might be fun. My first response was far from enthusiastic. But, in that way that wives have of being persuasive, I agreed to go along, albeit with more than a fair amount of cynicism. I was what we in the industry call a "drag along"—a euphemism that needs no explanation. After we'd wandered the lovely streets of historic Charleston (at one point in a hot, driving summer rain), listening to the guide spin ghost stories that wove history and real human beings into genuinely creepy tales, I was hooked. We then moved on to Savannah, where we enjoyed a haunted pub crawl, and again I was pleasantly surprised by how engaging an evening it was under the guidance of an experienced tour leader. At some point during our long drive back to Maryland, I turned to my wife and said, "We should do that in Annapolis." She agreed!

When we came home from vacation, I started doing research on the local legends and hauntings, and Ghosts of Annapolis Tours came into being shortly thereafter, offering walking tours and pub crawls that focused on sharing the stories of spirits who just cannot rest. In 2007, Julia Dray began working for me as a guide, the beginning of a partnership that led to the writing of our first book, *Haunted Annapolis: Ghosts of the Capital City*, published by The History Press in 2012. In 2014, the decision was finalized that it was time to expand our brand of tours and storytelling to nearby Baltimore, a city much in need of some historically accurate tours!

After doing just a little research, Fells Point was the logical choice. We've been scaring people ever since.

This, our second book, is the product of extensive research, interviews and personal investigations. The stories Julia and I have included are those that seemed most interesting to us, but these are not the only ghostly stories in Fells Point, let alone Baltimore as a whole—talk to a native and they might tell you about the ghost in their basement, or attic or bedroom. It's an old city, and there are a lot of ghosts.

We hope you'll come to Fells Point someday, and if you enjoy it enough, you can definitely stick around—lots of other people have…for the ages!

ACKNOWLEDGEMENTS

Mike Carter: I wish to thank my amazing family for all of their support, especially my son, Grayson, for his excitement over helping with my ghost tours, and my wife, Wendie, for being my muse and my sounding board over these many years. Thank you for keeping me on task from conception through tour script and finally to completed manuscript, for helping me focus my often scattered thoughts into cohesive ideas and, lastly, for dragging me on that first ghost tour in Charleston, South Carolina, and supporting me when I impulsively decided that I could create my own tours in Annapolis and again in Baltimore. Thank you, Sweetie!

Julia Dray: Dedicated to the residents of Fells Point—past, present and perpetual. And for Rob, who knows why.

INTRODUCTION

Not everyone believes in ghosts, but there are times when we are all afraid of the dark. The man who scoffs at tales of spectral apparitions still jumps at the sound of a stealthy footstep after midnight; the woman who declares such stories to be nonsense will nonetheless flinch from a shrouded figure behind the curtains. Children know the awful secrets that are held by dark and shadowed places. Monsters beneath the bed, feral clowns behind the curtains and fanged carnivores in the closet are just a small sample of their fears.

When the sun goes down, we grow wary. We fear the dangers that night conceals from us, and our senses strain to pick up the slightest concealed threat. Perhaps as a result, that's when ghosts most often walk.

Whether people are seeing an actual paranormal manifestation or experiencing some form of wish fulfillment, optical illusion or psychological breakdown is a matter of personal opinion, not science. The science behind paranormal investigation is largely based on instrument readings, and the sources of the electromagnetic fields or audible noises (or any of the many things paranormal researchers attempt to measure) cannot be determined with any scientific accuracy. Believers look at the evidence and see ghosts; deniers believe that a rational explanation has simply been overlooked. But even skeptics enjoy a good ghost story.

To a certain degree, we find it easy to identify with ghosts. They are our shadow selves, acting in a drama that is removed from us in time but not in substance. They are drunks, priests, harlots, innocent children or impoverished women; they are murderers and rapists and artists and bewildered foreigners. At some level, we can identify with their stories—we can understand how unfulfilled commitments, deeply held regrets or the trauma of awful violence could arrest a person's soul—locking them forever within one tiny space of time.

Ghost stories have a long tradition. One of the first ever recorded comes from a letter by Pliny the Younger, a Roman nobleman and legislator. Writing around AD 100, he recounted the story of a haunting in Athens, where a wealthy family was terrorized by the apparition of an emaciated and filthy man whose chains rattled and clanked as he moved about the house:

> *The afflicted inhabitants went without sleep at night, for fear of the unthinkable and dark terrors that could assail them. Lacking sleep, as has happened to many, their spirits were weakened and they fell into a kind of madness, which, as it increased, led them on the path to death. So weakened were they that even during the hours of daylight, when the ghost was not liable to appear, the very memory of their night terrors was so strong that it overtook their sight in every waking moment. They lived in fear constantly, even at those times that its source was absent.*[1]

The haunting was laid to rest by the philosopher Athenodorus, who purchased the house for a bargain price, undeterred by the tale of the ghost. On his very first evening in residence, he waited for the apparition's appearance, inquired what it wanted and then followed it into a courtyard. The ghost led him a short distance—and vanished. Marking the spot where it had disappeared, Athenodorus summoned a magistrate and arranged for an excavation. Several feet below the surface, they discovered the skeleton of a man wrapped in chains. Once the body had been properly set to rest, the haunting ceased.

Such resolutions of hauntings are common in ghost stories. Once the reason for remaining is gone, so is the ghost. There are many tales in which finding the body and burying it properly marks the end of paranormal activity—but not always. Some ghosts seem to haunt places that are perhaps quite far from where their bodies now lie, while others (as in one case described in this book) are said to rise from their burial sites to stroll the neighborhood.

Some ghosts are said to linger in search of justice or forgiveness or to convey a warning or important information. But other spirits seem to be driven by anger or malice, and they engage in violent acts and loud manifestations, apparently reveling in the fear that they inspire.

The ghosts of Fells Point are many. Some of them have been in residence for hundreds of years, described in local lore and even discussed in newspaper

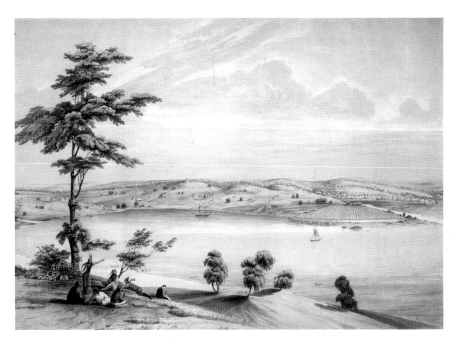

The Port of Baltimore in 1752. The city lagged behind Fells Point in the sale of lots and in population until the dawn of the eighteenth century. *New York Public Library.*

articles, while others have appeared in the last century. Some are pleasant to look at, while others are terrifying. Most are benign, but a few have driven people out of buildings, screaming as they run and refusing ever to return.

There are chance encounters on the streets and alleys, sudden apparitions that walk through walls or mount staircases in the air, unexpected visitors that knock on doors or appear in hallways or kitchens. There are the sounds of laughter, the loud jangle of jukebox music or a phonograph, the quiet murmur of intimate voices and the sharp metallic knives of screams. Doors slam, windows open, furniture moves, footsteps echo.

If this book included every location in which a door slammed shut unexpectedly, it would be a very long volume indeed. We have chosen to focus on hauntings that continue into the present day and are tied to significant buildings, historical events and specific individuals (where possible). It is our hope that by placing these ghosts within their own time and place, we can bring to life the history of one of Baltimore's most interesting neighborhoods, along with the fascinating people who have called it home—including a number who have simply refused to leave.

These are their stories.

1
A BRIEF HISTORY OF FELLS POINT

Here ships land their cargoes and here the crews wait not even for twilight to fly to the polluted arms of the white, black and yellow harlot.
—John David, a British visitor to Fells Point in 1798

The great depository of the hostile spirit of the United States against England.
—a description of Baltimore, and especially Fells Point, from the British press in 1814

It is said abroad that Baltimore is famous for three things: its' music, its' churches, its' military. Music is patronized by those who have the least ear, the best churches are built by the worst Christians and in the military department, it is observed that all logic is set at defiance in the making of majors out of minors.
—The Red Book of Baltimore

The people of Baltimore's Fells Point have played pivotal roles throughout American history: they smuggled gunpowder and supplies to George Washington's army, defeated British troops and survived a naval barrage during the War of 1812 and witnessed the first casualties of the American Civil War. The neighborhood has been scourged by epidemics and flooded with wave after wave of hopeful immigrants; its cobbled streets and ancient buildings have witnessed four hundred years of social upheaval, cultural trends and economic development.

The residents of Fells Point have a habit of resilience that has influenced the arc of American history. If it were not for the people of this tiny neighborhood, the story of the United States could have been very different.

A Passion for Gold

The area that became Fells Point was first charted by Captain John Smith in 1608, when he sailed north from the Virginia settlement at Jamestown to explore the huge bay to the north.[2] Smith was searching for a "Northwest Passage" that would allow ships to reach the Pacific Ocean and engage in trade with China and the Far East, and he was hoping to find gold—indeed, the investors in the Virginia colony, the London Company (or Virginia Company), were counting on it.

Spain's conquest and colonization of Mexico and Central America in the preceding century had sent staggering amounts of gold and silver into the coffers of the Spanish king, and English investors expected similar wealth from the northern continent. (What the company didn't know was that the Spanish had explored the Chesapeake in 1562, found no evidence of gold and left.)

Smith didn't find any gold either, but he made meticulous notes—his journals became the foundation on which settlers at Jamestown based their early explorations and settlements. Small trading posts, fishing villages and farms began to appear along the Chesapeake; the third-oldest English settlement in the United States (after Jamestown, Virginia, and Plymouth, Massachusetts) was founded on Kent Island by settlers from the Virginia Colony in 1631.

Over the course of two voyages in 1608–9, Smith created the first charts of what came to be called the Chesapeake Bay, and a branch of the Patapsco River, south of the modern city of Baltimore, is described in his journal from the first voyage.

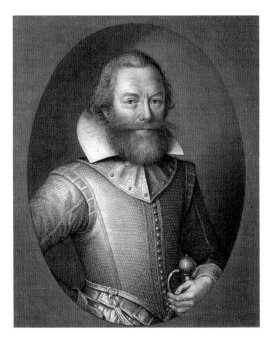

John Smith wrote several books about his explorations of the Chesapeake. He became a celebrity in England, and his descriptions of the New World also encouraged investors and would-be colonists. *New York Public Library.*

THE CREATION OF THE MARYLAND COLONY

Reports of the rich agricultural lands along the Chesapeake attracted much interest in Britain. When the London Company lost its charter in 1624, wealthy individuals and the Crown subsidized new settlements and sought charters for colonies. In 1631, George Calvert, First Baron of Baltimore, petitioned King Charles I for the creation of a colony to be called Maryland. As an English Roman Catholic, George Calvert had not been permitted to serve in any government post, and he designed a colony where all Christians could practice their faith, regardless of sect or denomination. Before the king could grant the charter, George Calvert died, and it was given instead to his twenty-four-year-old son Cecil.

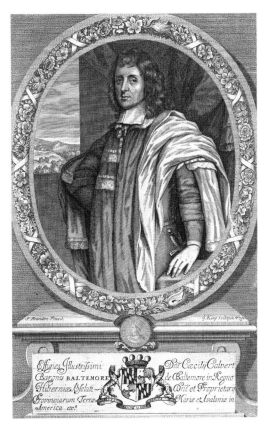

A carefully selected group, including Cecil's brother Leonard (who was appointed provincial governor), set sail in 1634 aboard the ships *Ark* and *Dove*. The settlers, a mix of Roman Catholic freemen and Protestant indentured servants (including Mathias de Sousa, the first African American in the Maryland colony), landed near the mouth of the Potomac River and set up a temporary camp on St. Clement's Island.[3] After negotiation with the local Native Americans, the colonists purchased land and began to erect the new capital: St. Mary's City. Over the next ten years, settlers began to spread north from the small foothold along the Potomac.

The colonial venture faced a number of challenges. One of the earliest came from Kent Island, which was now

Cecil Calvert carried his father's dream of a colony that offered religious liberty forward, beginning a long association between the Calvert family and Maryland. *New York Public Library.*

formally considered part of Maryland. The settlement, which had been founded by William Claiborne in 1631, saw itself as part of the Virginia colony, with Claiborne being the principal obstacle to a peaceful transition. Refusing to recognize Maryland's sovereignty, Claiborne even countenanced armed resistance, but he was expelled from the island in 1758. (The Virginia colony continued to litigate its legal right to the island until 1776.)

A greater danger to the colony was the question of religious freedom. By 1640, a number of Puritans had settled along the Chesapeake, where they agitated for the revocation of the religious freedoms guaranteed in the charter. They were emboldened by the 1649 execution of King Charles I, whose monarchy was succeeded by the Puritan "Commonwealth of England" under the leadership of Oliver Cromwell.

Leveraging their ideological connection to the new Lord Protector, Maryland Puritans harassed Parliament for repeal of the Maryland charter, while creating a lot of unrest within the colony itself, burning Catholic churches and harassing Catholic settlers. When the governor of Maryland passed an act ensuring religious liberty in 1649, it led to a brief civil war in 1655, in which the Calvert family briefly lost control of the colony. After the death of Lord Protector Oliver Cromwell in 1658, the restoration of the Stuart monarchy in England deprived Puritan colonists of vital support in Parliament. However, Puritan settlers far outnumbered Catholics, and intermittent episodes of religious strife continued to occur in the colony until the end of the seventeenth century.

JONESTOWN AND THE BIRTH OF BALTIMORE

In 1661, English colonist David Jones ventured north along the Chesapeake Bay; upon reaching the Patapsco River, he located a stream that tumbled down a steady incline until it met the river. Recognizing the potential of the site, Jones built a watermill on the "fall line."* As new settlers arrived, the mill complex became the nucleus for "Jones Town," a small settlement that was later incorporated into Baltimore City. While Jones Falls was among the first, the hills above what is now Baltimore's Inner Harbor were soon filled with high-volume grain mills that turned Maryland wheat into flour destined for the West Indies and beyond.

---

* The "fall line" on a waterway is generally considered to be the point at which boats traveling upstream cannot continue without portaging rapids or waterfalls and where there is the most power to be obtained from the rushing water. In Baltimore, the fall line lies between the hard rock of the Appalachian Piedmont and the softer sedimentary rocks of the Atlantic Coastal Plain.

Grain was an important commodity, but it paled in comparison to another colonial crop. The English had not found gold in their new colonies, but the temperate mid-Atlantic colonies possessed abundant quantities of natural tobacco, which proved nearly as valuable. The profits from tobacco were enormous, and as the habit of smoking caught on throughout the world, the market exploded.[4]

In 1694, the colonial capital was moved north, to an originally Puritan settlement on the banks of the Severn River. Ann Arundel's Town, later to become Annapolis, was more centrally located, easily reachable from Maryland's Eastern Shore and from towns and settlements to the

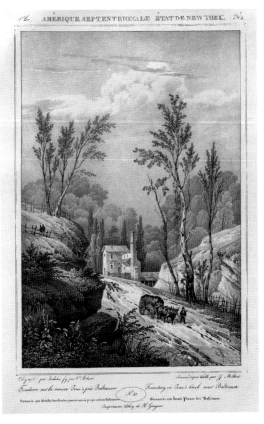

Mills on the Jones Falls. A rapid drop in elevation offered an inexhaustible supply of power for the grain mills that sprang up around the Port of Baltimore. *New York Public Library.*

west. As tobacco and grain flowed into the market from a constantly increasing number of Maryland and Virginia plantations, the need for an administered and supervised port grew.

The Maryland General Assembly created the Port of Baltimore in 1706. Thirty miles northwest of Annapolis, the site was convenient to the grain mills along the fall line and the tobacco warehouses, while the deep waters of the Patapsco River provided a sheltered anchorage for ships.

Originally, the official Port encompassed only "the Basin," a marshy scoop of land that is today's Inner Harbor. Deep-water ships could not navigate the shallow waters to reach the Basin and were forced to anchor out in the Patapsco. Tobacco and milled flour were moved in flat-bottomed barges from the warehouses, which began just off a

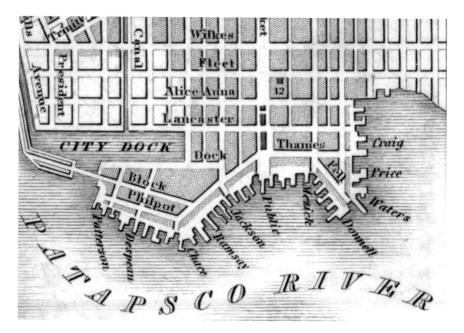

The wharves and harbor area of Fells Point, 1790. *New York Public Library.*

narrow hook of land to the north and east of the Basin. In early years, this spit of land was called "the Hook," but in the 1730s, it acquired a new name.[5]

THE FELLS OF FELLS POINT

The Fells came from Ulverton, a small town in the northwest English county of Lancashire. A modestly well-to-do family, they had strong ties to George Fox, founder of the Society of Friends (also known as the Quakers), and it was the connection to this community that encouraged the immigration of Edward and William Fell. The Maryland colony had a small, but prosperous, Quaker population. Edward Fell, who arrived in 1728, settled into the community, invested in land around Jones Town and opened a store. When William arrived in 1730, Edward gave his younger brother some advice as to where he should build his shipyard: he suggested that William purchase the Hook.

The property comprised nearly eighty acres and offered deep-water anchorage on the north eastern side, where William constructed docks and his shipyard. The southwestern portion of the property fronted on the shallower water along Baltimore's inner harbor, which was crowded with barges that transferred cargoes to merchant ships forced to anchor out far from the docks. The warehouses Fell built along that side of the Hook were quickly filled with merchandise that could then be loaded onto ships that tied up at his deep-water docks. Prosperity followed quickly, and in 1732, William Fell married Sarah Bond, the daughter of his London-trained attorney, John Bond.

Baltimore County, *January* 4, 1762.

NOTICE is hereby given to all Perfons who have taken, or fubfcribed their Names for Lots of Ground, according to the Number, in a late Plan for a Town joining *Patapfco* River, in faid County, Near *Baltimore-Town*, Maryland, on a Point known by the Name of *Fell's Point*, That their Leafes are now ready to be filled up, and that constant Attendance will be given, at the House of the Subscriber on said Point, till the Twentieth Day of April next, in Order to execute such Leases, and that all Persons so subscribing their Names for Lots, and refufing or neglecting to take Leafes for them till the *21st* Day of April next, their Subscription will be looked upon as void and of no effect, and the Lots fo refufed or neglected will be offered to others.

EDWARD FELL.

Edward Fell began the sale of lots but died shortly afterward, leaving his wife, Ann Bond Fell, to carry on with the sales. This is a reproduction of the original notice. Maryland Gazette *Archives.*

The young couple lived on a property called "Fells Prospect," and it was in this house that Sarah gave birth to their only child, whom they named after his uncle Edward.

By the 1750s, trade had grown to such an extent that new docks, warehouses and supportive industries (rope-walks, ship's chandlers and so on) were desperately needed. The notion of a town at Fells Point was gaining momentum, but William was reluctant to sell any of his land; ultimately, it was William's son who undertook the project of surveying the property.

In 1758, young Edward Fell married his mother's niece, a strong-willed young woman named Ann Bond. The couple built a home on present-day Shakespeare Street; in the next year they had a son, named William for his paternal grandfather. Just prior to the elder William's death in 1762, the family offered lots for sale in the new town. Edward Fell placed an advertisement in the *Maryland Gazette* on January 14, 1762, notifying those who had submitted their names for the right to purchase lots in his new town that "lea[s]es are now ready to be filled up." The location is given as near "Baltimore-Town, Maryland, on a Point known by the Name of Fells-Point."

By 1766, many lots were sold and more sales pending, when Edward Fell died suddenly at the age of thirty. Sales came to a halt while his will was proved, and many feared that the equally new town of Baltimore (which had joined with the neighboring Jones Town in 1745) would poach impatient buyers.

Following probate of the will, Ann Bond Fell proceeded with the land sales, enjoying such success that several Baltimore landowners started a smear campaign against her, blackening her reputation and attempting to cast doubt on the legitimacy of the land titles. Ann's grandfather, Baltimore lawyer John Bond, advertised in local publications, denouncing the slurs and vouching for the legality of the titles. The sales continued with such speed that houses and businesses rose along the streets of Ann's town long before Baltimore began to come together—all the lots in Fells Point were sold by 1773.

In addition to warehouses, chandleries (ship supplies), shipyards and docks, Fells Point boasted many fine homes and sizable commercial buildings. The oldest residence in Baltimore is the Robert Long House at 812 South Ann Street, built in 1765. The Waterfront Hotel, built in 1771, is the second-oldest brick building in the city, and several of the buildings that now comprise part of the modern Admiral Fell Inn date to 1770. In that same year, John Cantrell built the London Coffee House on Thames Street, the oldest surviving commercial structure in Baltimore.

Two Very Different Towns

Baltimore and Fells Point emerged from the American Revolution as two distinct towns, each with its own customs and social atmosphere. Although they were a scant mile apart, the population of Baltimore remained only half that of Fells Point until the early years of the nineteenth century. Baltimore was the home of wealthy merchants and landowners; etchings of "downtown" in the early years of the eighteenth century show a scattering of stately homes set well away from the water's edge, with a small ruff of docks along the shallow shore of the Basin. Fells Point was far less refined; it teemed with small shops, rooming houses, warehouses and modest residences, while the crowded wharves seethed with activity night and day. The Jones Falls was the dividing line.

During the American Revolution, Fells Point earned a reputation as a major shipyard. The famous "Baltimore Clippers" came out of Fells Point; with their sharply raked (tilted) two-masted design and a narrow hull that sliced through water, the ships could outrun nearly any other frigate (the

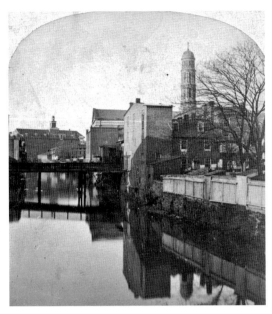

Bridges over the Jones Falls near Fells Point, 1880. The natural dividing line between Fells Point and Baltimore, it is now almost completely hidden beneath the city streets. *New York Public Library.*

ship was also known as the "Yankee Racehorse"). The privateer *Chasseur*, built in the Point by Thomas Kemp, was responsible for the capture or destruction of many British vessels in the War of 1812.[6] Burned out of his Portsmouth shipbuilding yards by the British, shipwright David Stodder relocated to Baltimore and built the USS *Constellation*, originally a thirty-six-gun frigate, in his Fells Point shipyards in 1797. It was one of many U.S. Navy vessels to emerge from the Point. The shipyards and associated businesses (including numerous brothels and unsavory drinking spots) bustled with activity—by the 1790s, 34 percent of the inhabitants of Fells Point were involved in building, fitting and sailing ships.

Fells Point was also a depot for international trade, by virtue of its deep-water anchorage. Goods manufactured in Baltimore had to be taken by wagon or barge from the harbor and transferred to warehouses along Fells Point, where they awaited shipment. Africans destined for slavery were also warehoused along the Point upon arrival; to avoid outraging the numerous Quakers in the community, slave traders typically moved them through the streets in covered carts in the middle of the night. The complicated business of taxes and stamps, and even insurance, was another cog in the Point's economic gears. But the physical proximity between Baltimore and Fells Point made it inevitable that they should be joined.

In 1794, the Maryland legislature authorized the incorporation of Fells Point with Baltimore, but opposition from the local merchants delayed it until the two towns were finally joined on January 1, 1797.

THE NAPOLEONIC WARS

Or the War of 1812

Many Americans do not realize that their War of 1812 was just a small war within a string of larger conflicts between European powers. Starting in 1803, when France's Napoleon Bonaparte tried to hamstring Great Britain's trade power by restricting its access to Europe's marketplaces, the wars ground on until 1815, when Napoleon was finally neutralized at Waterloo by a coalition force of British, Germans, Belgians, Dutch and Prussians under the command of the Duke of Wellington. Roughly three and a half million combatants died on battles and naval conflicts throughout Europe, compared to the approximately twenty thousand who lost their lives in North America during the battles of the War of 1812.

Early in the conflict, Great Britain tried to control international trade through a series of "Orders in Council." These Orders outlined British demands for the behavior of neutral shipping, decreed a blockade of French ports (as well as those of Napoleon's allies) and allowed for the forcible seizure and re-enlistment of sailors who deserted British service.

While the trade restrictions were infuriating, what really made Americans angry was the seizure of American seamen who were then forcibly enlisted in the Royal Navy. Because American shipping was neutral, many British deserters took jobs on ships flying the U.S. flag. Desperately short of sailors, British warships stopped and searched American merchant ships. The United States recognized British-born sailors on American-flagged ships as American citizens. Great Britain did not, and its ships seized not only British-born sailors but also any suspicious passenger.[7]

The United States formally declared war against another nation for the first time in its history on June 18, 1812, when both houses of Congress approved a bill to declare hostilities against Great Britain, which President James Madison signed. Ironically, the British Foreign Minister, Lord Castlereagh, had authorized the repeal of the offending Orders on June 23—but word didn't reach Washington until several weeks later, and by that time, U.S. general William Huff's army was invading Upper Canada (modern southern Ontario).

Most of the land battles occurred in British Canada, along the Great Lakes and in what were called the "Northwest Territories" (now Ohio, Illinois, Kentucky and Indiana), but it was the largely unwitnessed actions at sea that cost the British the most men and materiel.

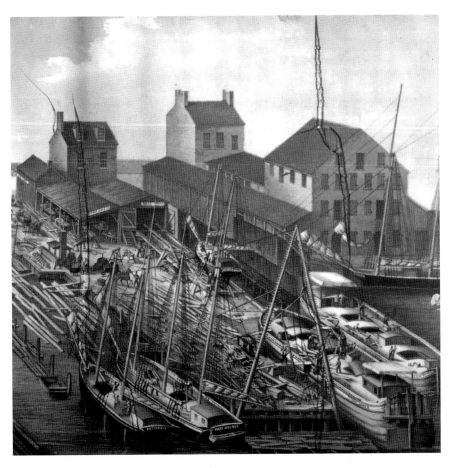

Fells Point shipyards, circa 1820. *Author archive.*

Throughout the War of 1812, the shipyards of Fells Point turned out a number of ships operating under "letters of marque" from the U.S. government. These letters gave a ship's captain the legal authority to attack and seize British ships and cargoes, which were then auctioned off for the profit of both the government and the ship's company. The profits could be staggering, and a number of American vessels set out to hunt down British merchant ships as they crossed the Atlantic. In a two-year span, fifty-six privateer vessels built in Fells Point captured or destroyed over five hundred British vessels. One of the most famous of the Fells Point privateers, Captain Thomas Boyle, raided British coastal shipping and gave a document to one of the captured ship captains that proclaimed an American naval blockade of Great Britain.[8]

The British had to pull ships out of the fleet—which was blockading Napoleon's ports—and send them back to guard the coastline from the American ships that originated in Fells Point. Parliament, public and press demanded that the "nest of pirates" be destroyed. One speech in Parliament referenced a recent victory against the Danish: "The truculent inhabitants [of Fells Point] must be tamed with those weapons that shook the wooden turrets of Copenhagen!"

Prepared to strike a decisive blow, a British fleet was sent into the Chesapeake Bay. In the middle of August 1814, troops attacked and burned Washington, D.C. (famously pausing to dine at the White House before setting it afire). The attack on the U.S. capital was retaliation for the American destruction of Fort York in British Canada, but the British had another loss to avenge as well. Leaving a smoldering city in its wake, the fleet raised anchor and sailed north to destroy the shipyards of Fells Point.

The Battle of North Point began on September 12, 1814, three weeks after the burning of Washington. The British intended a two-pronged assault: five thousand soldiers under Major General Robert Ross were to land at North Point and move south and west to attack the city from the undefended northeast, while naval vessels began a bombardment of Fort

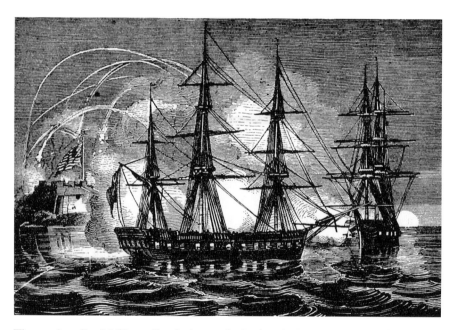

The attack on Fort McHenry. Despite hours of relentless shelling, the hastily reinforced fortifications around Baltimore's harbor held off the British attack. *New York Public Library.*

McHenry in the hope of breaching the harbor defenses and landing marines to set fires in the center city.

But the British underestimated how fiercely the inhabitants would defend their homes—the people of Baltimore had gone to work the moment they heard about the burning of Washington, building fortifications and amassing volunteers. General Ross was killed on the first day, and Maryland troops threw back the British landing at North Point, forcing them to retreat to their ships. After much deliberation, the British commanders decided to focus on destroying Fort McHenry with a naval bombardment, with the aim of landing troops amid the chaos.

In the midst of a horrific thunderstorm on the evening of September 13, nineteen massed British vessels commenced a bombardment that rivaled the thunder. South Baltimore "shook with the cannon," one witness declared, and throughout the night no one knew whether the fortifications still stood. As the dawn light stole through the fading clouds of the storm and the acrid smoke from the cannons, Francis Scott Key looked out from a British ship sitting farther out on the Patapsco and saw the American flag waving defiantly above the ramparts of Fort McHenry. The failure of the assault was obvious to the British, and they withdrew. The fleet sailed to the south, toward a final defeat at the hand of Andrew Jackson at the Battle of New Orleans in 1815.

The People of Fells Point

Most of the early settlers were English colonists (the blue-collar Scots and Welsh didn't start showing up in serious numbers until much later, mostly in the early nineteenth century), but from the beginning, the population was a mix of nationalities.

They included Dutch merchants buying goods for settlements in Delaware and eastern Maryland, Spanish slave factors, Portuguese traders and a whole lot of French. Two successive waves of French-speaking immigrants settled in Baltimore and Fells Point. After 1763, at least eight thousand French expelled from English Canada built homes in what's still called Frenchtown. (A larger group of refugees went much farther south and are now known as the "Cajuns" of Louisiana.) In 1793, over fifty ships arrived from Haiti, bearing French settlers fleeing the slave revolution.

Beginning in 1815, waves of German immigration began—to the point that there were three German-language churches in Fells Point by 1830.

Polish immigrants started showing up in 1840–60, building churches and meeting halls throughout the Point; large numbers of Italian and Irish arrived in the late nineteenth and early twentieth centuries, along with a substantial number of European Jews. And through the years, merchants and sailors from every part of the world settled in the town—one of the rope walk managers in 1790 was Russian, and several shipping managers had Greek and Arabic surnames.

But by far the largest number of immigrants came from Africa. Fells Point was a trans-shipment point for Africans who survived the dreadful voyage across the Atlantic; warehouses on the Broadway pier were used for holding and trading slaves for use on the farms and plantations of Maryland's interior. But some slaves were purchased by residents of Fells Point, who trained them in a variety of shipbuilding skills that allowed them to earn their freedom.

By 1830, one out of every six workers in the Fells Point shipyards was African American. Most worked as "caulkers," where speed and skill could earn wages that matched or surpassed their white counterparts. The freedmen in Fells Point formed the Association of Black Caulkers in 1838 and were unafraid to strike for better wages—sometimes even going so far as to actively sabotage ships. By 1840, one in five Baltimore residents was of African descent, but nearly half of those people were free men and women. There were five schools and at least six churches for the free community listed in the 1841 directory.[9]

THE CIVIL WAR

Baltimore was torn by internal strife in the years that led up to the American Civil War. In fact, some historians say that the first Union casualties of the Civil War were taken in the streets of Fells Point on April 19, 1861.

The town was a hotbed of secessionist activity—Abraham Lincoln received only 1,100 of the more than 30,000 votes cast in the 1860 election, and the threat of assassination was so great that he traveled secretly through Baltimore on the way to his inauguration in February 1861. Secessionists and unionists alike formed armed militias in support of their ideals; the secessionists called themselves the "National Volunteers," while the unionists appropriated the name "Minute Men." The *Fanny Crenshaw*, a small ship from Virginia, inflamed tensions by flying a secessionist flag in Fells Point; a

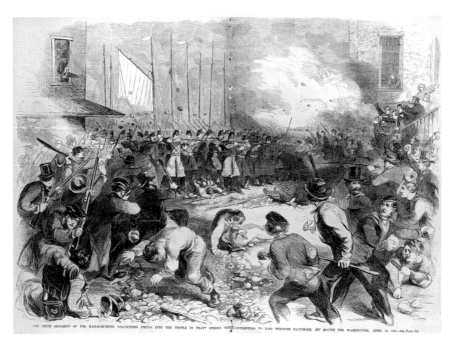

Southern sympathizers attacked the Sixth Massachusetts as it traveled through Baltimore in 1861. Four soldiers died; some consider them the first military casualties of the American Civil War. *Library of Congress.*

pro-unionist mob stormed the ship, tore down the flag and threw the ship's boy in the water. The stage was set for conflict, and when Union troops began to move through the city on their way to fortify Washington, D.C., the pot boiled over.

There were several train lines that ended in Baltimore but no central station; railcars that needed to transfer between stations were pulled down Pratt Street by horse-drawn rail. (Steam engines were not allowed on the streets of the city.)

Troops from the Sixth Massachusetts Militia arrived at the President Street Station and began the transfer to Camden Station, ten blocks to the west. Several carloads managed the trip without undue incident, but then a mob assembled and began to pelt the cars with paving stones and other missiles. The railway to Pratt Street blocked, the troops formed up and began to march toward Camden Station. The mob attacked the rear companies of the regiment, and shots were fired. The soldiers fired back, triggering an all-out battle between the troops, Union supporters, Southern sympathizers and the Baltimore police. Four soldiers and twelve civilians were killed in the fighting; Corporal Sumner Needham is sometimes considered the first Union casualty of the Civil War.

As a result of the riot, the harbor was closed and martial law declared in the city of Baltimore (which remained in effect for nearly the entirety of the war). Many leading citizens who supported the South were temporarily imprisoned at Fort McHenry. Native Marylander James Ryder Randall, a teacher in Louisiana, moved by the loss of a friend in the riots, wrote "Maryland, My Maryland" for the Southern cause; despite its Confederate provenance, seventy-six years later it became the state's official song.

After the Civil War

Fells Point continued to be a center of shipbuilding throughout the nineteenth century, turning out the swift and graceful Baltimore Clippers, but the advent of steam engines marked the end of the industry—the harbor was too choked by silt to accommodate the deeper draught of the metal ships—even though the natives had been dredging it regularly since 1785, using what was called a "mud machine."[10] Fells Point turned to new industries that allowed it to take advantage of the cheap labor of immigrants.

The farmland to the west of Baltimore and the broad fields of the Eastern Shore produced in abundance, and the canneries of the city turned that produce into gold. When barges arrived laden with fresh vegetables, a whistle would sound and the workers (mostly women) would stream in, working until the barges were empty and the freshly labeled cans ready to ship.

The men labored at the steel plants and machinery shops or worked the water as bargemen or longshoremen. Others worked at the rail yards that connected Baltimore to the cities of the Midwest and the Eastern Seaboard.

By the middle of the twentieth century, Baltimore was an industrial city. The once-teeming waters around the harbor were a stew of toxic chemicals and foul-smelling sludge. Fells Point became just another semi-industrial area that was pockmarked with bars, deteriorating houses and plagued by crime and poverty.

It took the threat of total destruction to jump-start a change in the neighborhood. In the 1970s, plans for a new expressway along the waterfront brought together a coalition of long-term residents and passionate newcomers whose protests stalled the project until they managed to get Fells Point added to the National Register of Historic Places. This designation

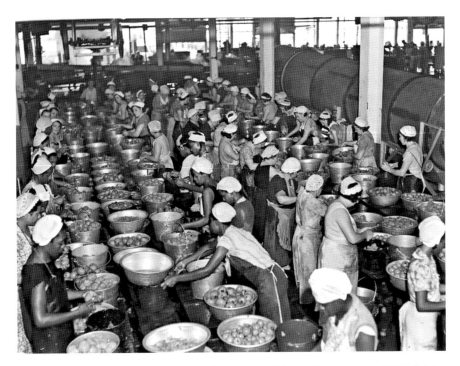

Although racial segregation was common in many workplaces, the canneries of Fells Point didn't have time for that—when fresh produce arrived, it had to be processed immediately. *New York Public Library.*

prevented the use of federal funds for the road project and contributed to the project's cancellation. Barbara Mikulski, a Fells Point native and later U.S. senator, was one of the leaders of the protests.

By the year 2000, Fells Point's popularity as a destination had grown to the point that it was (and is!) one of the "must see" neighborhoods of Baltimore. Visitors enjoy the juxtaposition of building styles, the historic nature of the buildings and the robust vigor of the street life. Many historic buildings have been repurposed as restaurants or inns and serve a new generation of customers while housing a population of shadowy and historic inhabitants that never wanted to leave.

2

THE PERILOUS LIFE OF A SAILOR

Those who would go to sea for pleasure, would go to hell for a pastime.
—Eighteenth-century aphorism

Being in a ship is being in jail, with the chance of being drowned.
—Samuel Johnson

In 1800, Fells Point had sixteen shipyards and was building some of the best ships under sail, but once the War of 1812 showed the importance of Baltimore and Fells Point to the American maritime industry, the town exploded. By 1833, Baltimore was one of the three largest ports in the country, and sailors washed in and out with the tide.

In constant danger of death from an unforgiving sea, an eighteenth- or nineteenth-century sailor was also at the mercy of a commander whose powers were absolute; a merchant captain's word was law for all who signed the ship's articles (a written agreement that stated the terms of employment), and service in a nation's navy meant sailing under a man who could flog, starve, torture and kill with full legal authority. Mutiny—the act of overthrowing the legally designated authority on a ship—was uncommon but not rare. The punishment for an unsuccessful mutiny was often death, and successful challenges to authority were few; those that succeeded often saw the vessel in question change sides in a conflict or turn pirate.[11]

So it was only natural that sailors took the opportunity to "cut loose" once they were free of their ship. The taverns, gambling dens and brothels of

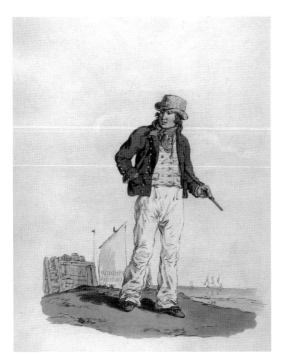

Ordinary sailors wore a basic uniform of white duck trousers, a blue-and-white-checked shirt and a blue jacket. *New York Public Library.*

Fells Point echoed with the shouts of mariners, whose drunken exploits and rowdy behavior made respectable hotels unwilling to take their business.

An old song asks the question "What do you do with a drunken sailor?" and the answers are usually humorous, like "put him in bed with the captain's daughter." But there are lots of other things you can do with a drunken sailor: "hit him in the head and take his money," "roll him in the street until he's bloody," "knock him in the nob and take him sailing." All of these verses refer to the less amusing things that could happen to an incapacitated seaman; he could be robbed, assaulted, murdered or kidnapped.

The custom of "press-ganging" sailors was common in Great Britain and to some extent in the colonies. Officers of Royal Navy vessels would descend on port taverns with a crew of cudgel-bearing sailors and grab every drunken seaman they could find—those who tried to escape through a rear exit usually found another crew waiting in the darkness of the alley. It was easy to "cosh"* a drunken sailor; hit from behind, the seaman could then be carried onto the ship just like any drunken sailor returning from shore leave. But if the cosh hit at the wrong angle or was swung too hard, the results could be fatal for the unlucky sailor.

The almost equally unlucky survivors would be "pressed" into service, forced to join the navy for an enlistment that was not only brutal and ill-paid but also often fatal. Maritime law made him a captive the moment

---

* A cosh was a thick cudgel with a weighted and padded end (usually a sand-filled leather or oilcloth bag); "coshing" someone meant administering a blow to the back of the head.

he signed the ship's articles. American maritime law was in many ways no different from that in Great Britain; until the late nineteenth century, whether it was real or forged, a sailor's signature on a ship's articles formed a legally binding contract that extended until the end of a specified voyage.

The U.S. Navy seldom resorted to press-ganging save during wartime, but captains of merchant vessels and deep-water fishing vessels—trapped at anchor because of an inadequate crew—often did.

A ship's officers simply outsourced the work of finding unwilling labor to gangs known as "crimpers," which prowled harbors, searching for vulnerable seamen. Because no respectable hotel would have them, visiting sailors were forced to rent rooms over taverns or gambling establishments, where they were easy prey for the crimpers, who took "blood money" for each sailor clubbed or drugged unconscious and delivered to a ship. The prostitutes in the brothels were often accomplices, selling an insensate customer after looting his wallet and appropriating most of his clothes for resale.

Many a man woke up on a ship that was heading out to sea, sold into an uncertain term of maritime slavery. The luckier victims of "crimping" were paid out in full at the end of the voyage; the unlucky were killed and thrown overboard or abandoned in a penniless condition, far from home. Reportedly, kidnapping crew to work a fishing ship was not an uncommon occurrence (until well into the twentieth century), and in the best situations, the unwilling crew member was put back on dry land with some money in his pockets—in the worst, he was killed on the voyage back to port and his body thrown overboard.

In 1825, religious activists in the temperance movement took the first steps toward providing sailors a safe place to berth while they were ashore in Baltimore. They built the Seamen's Union Bethel, a church that fronted on the harbor, and also operated a boardinghouse right next door where sailors were safe but required to remain sober (temperate) and attend religious services.[12]

There were quite a number of sailors who took advantage of the Seaman's Bethel (in spite of having to remain sober), and local temperance advocates did their best to eliminate legal and illegal sales of alcohol. (Many boardinghouse landlords supplemented their rents by selling liquor.) But there were still plenty of taverns and drinking places, and as Fells Point's usefulness as a harbor diminished after the Civil War, the shift from bustling port to seedy waterfront began—an 1888 report listed 323 saloons in Fells Point.

The Seamen's Bethel Church building and its boardinghouse stood at 1621 Thames Street and provided a place of safety until after the Civil War, when the building was sold to a private buyer. Baltimore operated under martial law for the duration of the war, and the streets of the port areas were patrolled regularly. It's possible that they became so safe that the Seaman's Bethel was no longer necessary. But once the war ended, the unwary sailor was again in danger, and a new facility was opened to provide a safe haven: the Port Mission, a large building at the corner of Broadway and Thames Streets.

One Haunted Hotel: The Admiral Fell Inn

Broadway and Thames Streets

There never was an Admiral Fell (at least none related to the family who settled the Point). But even a historian who likes to stick to facts can enjoy the whimsy of the name, which also manages to express the maritime focus of the area in which the hotel and restaurant are located.

The inn is composed of eight interconnected preexisting buildings and a three-story addition that was built in 1994. The oldest of the buildings dates to 1770, with the remainder ranging from 1791 to 1890; most of these held ground-floor shops with living quarters on the floors above. In the 1830s, one of these row homes contained Henry Colburn's stationery store and circulating library, and another was the workshop of Levi Cromwell, a lock and gunsmith.

The first recorded use of the property at the corner of Broadway and Thames was as a livery stable, owned and operated by Edward Johnson, mayor of Baltimore during the War of 1812 and the man who organized much of the city's defenses during the British attack. By 1830, Willard Post had opened the Union Coffee House on the same lot; customers could sip their coffee and look across the street at the Seamen's Union Bethel, with its safe beds and Christian welcome for visiting sailors. But the coffeehouse was replaced by a new establishment after the Civil War.

In 1881, the Port Mission Women's Auxiliary opened the doors on a building where it planned "to maintain under Christian influence a boarding house for seamen, a home away from home, a social and recreational center where the seafarer might find a safe refuge while in port." The boardinghouse later expanded to an adjoining building, and the remaining lots on Broadway were purchased and incorporated as well.

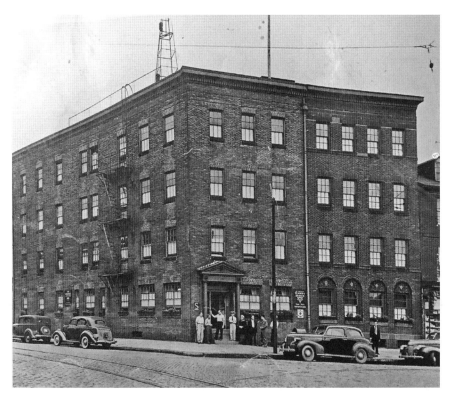

The Anchorage, circa 1925. The building's location in the heart of Fells Point's harbor district was central to its mission of offering safe refuge for visiting sailors. *Admiral Fell Inn.*

The central building of what is now the landmark Admiral Fell Inn was opened on December 3, 1900. Known as the "Anchorage," it had a restaurant, reading/writing room, baggage storage room, lobby and dormitories that could accommodate a total of 152 sailors in spaces so tiny that the guests referred to the accommodations as "the doghouse." Although the rooms were small, they were clean, and many seamen regarded the Anchorage as a home away from home, even to the extent of having their mail forwarded there. A sailor who was down on his luck could have a room and three meals a day for the price of his labor in the laundry or kitchen; an injured mariner could receive medical attention from the mission's volunteers. Most importantly, residence at the mission greatly reduced the chances of being "shanghaied," a term that came into use in the 1850s that referred to the fact that kidnapped crew members often wound up in that Chinese port city.

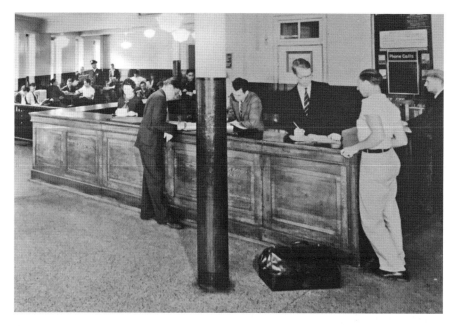

The lobby of the Anchorage. Sailors often had their mail sent to the mission, where it was held for them until they arrived back in port. *Admiral Fell Inn.*

In September 1918, soldiers at Fort George C. Meade began to fall ill; within a few days, nearly two thousand soldiers on the base had been diagnosed with influenza, and there were many cases at Fort McHenry and Aberdeen Proving Ground. Although the infection was at first confined to these military bases, civilian workers carried it back to the neighborhoods of Baltimore.

Unlike most strains of influenza, which claim the lives of the weakest but often spare the young and strong, this one killed healthy young adults. Worldwide, five hundred million people were sickened by the H1N1 influenza pandemic, and it is estimated that fifty to one hundred million people died—between 3 and 6 percent of the world's population. When the pandemic ended, only one region on the entire planet had not reported an outbreak: the isolated island of Marajo in Brazil's Amazon River Delta. In Baltimore, nearly twenty-five thousand people were afflicted, and there were over four thousand deaths by the end of 1918.

With hospitals packed to capacity, any available building was opened as an infirmary, and infected sailors wound up in buildings operated by charities such as the Port Mission Women's Auxiliary. Even with careful nursing, the crowded wards and the respiratory nature of the disease

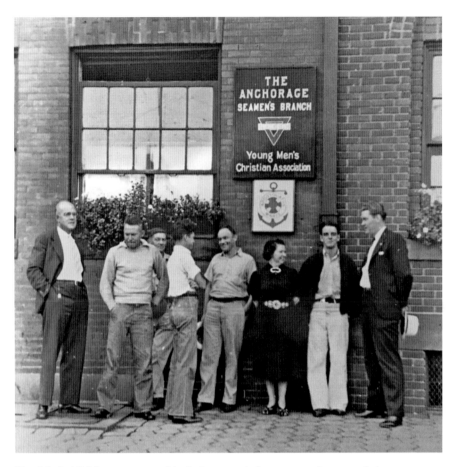

The Admiral Fell Inn was restored in the late twentieth century and once again hosts guests from around the world—but in much more luxurious accommodations. *Admiral Fell Inn.*

meant that many victims did not survive; there is no way to know how many lives came to an end in the tiny rooms of the Anchorage, but the total was probably in the hundreds, including at least six of the volunteer nurses.

After the epidemic subsided, the Anchorage continued to operate as a seaman's hotel, and the Port Mission passed management of the facility to the Young Men's Christian Association (YMCA) in 1929. Renamed the "Baltimore Seamen's Branch of the YMCA," the facility offered 105 tiny rooms that could be rented for just thirty-five cents a night—but guests had to bathe, stay sober and promise to behave.

The last documented case of shanghaiing took place in Fells Point in 1945—within sight of the Seaman's Branch. But with the end of World War

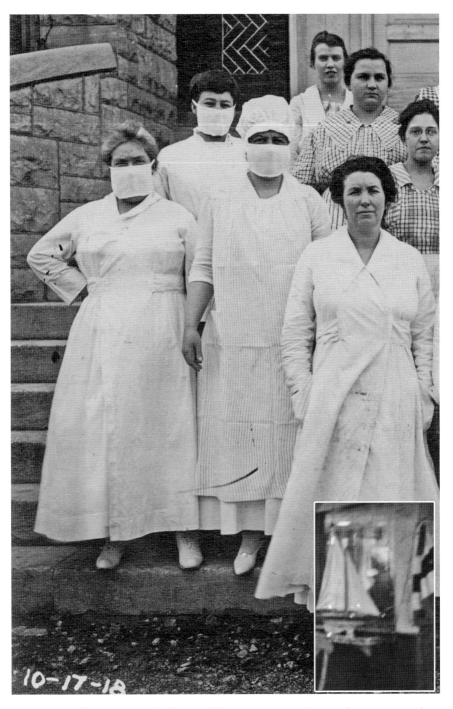

10-17-18

A customer taking a picture of a ship model (*inset*) captured the image of a woman wearing clothing similar to that of nurses during the epidemic. *Admiral Fell Inn.*

ll spelling a further decline of Baltimore shipping, the YMCA closed its doors in 1955. The building became a vinegar bottling plant, but by 1980, it was a derelict shell. (The restaurant of the current inn is located in what was once the main distilling room.)

In 1985, the building reopened after a complete renovation. As the Admiral Fell Inn, it operates a bed-and-breakfast with eighty rooms after a 1996 expansion that incorporated existing buildings as well as new construction. Once the inn was open for business, both staff and customers began to report encounters with ghostly figures or strange phenomena—so many that several serious paranormal investigations have taken place on site, and it has been featured in various television programs.

There are many spirits that haunt the Admiral Fell Inn, but no one has yet been able to put a name to any of them. No one knows why a sailor sits on the window ledge outside one room or why a woman walks through the wall of room 218…but quite a few witnesses say that they do. Many of the ghosts are women, dressed in sober clothing and making notes on clipboards—the lingering spirits of the brave ladies of the Port Mission who lost their lives as they cared for the people of their community and sailors far from home.

- In one second-floor room (number unknown), a dog woke his owners several times by barking and scratching at the frame of a window. Finally, the man staying in the room got up and looked out of the window to see a man dressed as a nineteenth-century sailor sitting on the window ledge; the sailor turned and looked at him before disappearing. On another occasion during that visit, the dog began barking and scratching at the door of the room, desperate to leave. The owners put him on a leash and let him lead wherever he wanted to go, which happened to be a spot just around the corner on Shakespeare Street. He sat directly in front of a small yard; through the bars of the fence, the visitors saw the stone marker for the Fell family graveyard.

- A guest in room 218, a scientist in town to work on a project at Johns Hopkins University, was a determined skeptic of the paranormal. He was forced to question his sanity after being awakened by creaking floorboards in time to witness the apparition of a woman standing at the foot of his bed holding what looked like a medical chart, onto which she was making notations. She looked at him inquisitively, then back down at the chart before turning and walking through his hotel room wall. He chalked the incident up as a waking dream, but the next morning, he was plagued by questions and went down to the front desk. Reluctantly, he told his story and described the woman to the manager on duty, who directed him to a book in the hotel's reading area that contained photographs from the hotel's history. As the guest flipped through the pages, one photograph caught his eye: a woman in a long dark dress covered by a white apron, her hair swept up beneath a white cap—the very woman who had appeared at the foot of his bed. One of the volunteers at the Port Mission, the young woman had worked as a nurse during the Spanish flu epidemic—and was, perhaps, another victim of it.

- Another apparition of a nurse has been reported in the basement of the hotel, which now houses the Tavern at the Admiral. During the Spanish flu epidemic, this part of the building held cold-storage facilities and was pressed into service as a morgue. Many people have reported seeing a woman wearing a white cap and apron or hearing brisk footsteps and the rustle of skirts in an empty room. A patron who took a photo in the bar was shocked to find a woman standing behind a display of ship models, her dark uniform and nurse's cap clearly visible. As of this writing, bartenders in the Tavern are more than happy to share a copy of that photograph with customers—stop in for a beer and check it out!

- One of the housekeeping staff reported being touched and feeling cold spots on several different occasions while working in room 413. She said it felt as though a slight breeze was blowing against her face or arms, like someone had walked close by her. She also reported feeling as though someone had put a hand on her shoulder; many guests in the room have reported similar phenomena.

- In September 2003, during Hurricane Isabel, guests of the inn were evacuated to safety, but the manager and several others stayed behind in the lobby to wait out the storm. During the evening, the group went for dinner, leaving an assistant manager in the lobby to keep watch and listen for the phones. When they returned, the manager nervously reported hearing a lot of noise, footsteps and loud talking in the rooms directly above the lobby, but when they went to investigate, the rooms were empty and undisturbed. On the following evening, another manager reported the same phenomena and added that he could see the ceiling above vibrate with the pounding of dancing feet. It sounded like one heck of a party, and staff still joke that the ghosts took advantage of the empty building to throw a "hurricane party" of their own.

- Guests have called to complain about a loud gathering in the room above or to one side of their own, but the laughing and music and occasional shouts, mixed with the heavy tread of dancing feet, come to an end the moment the call to the front desk is placed. The guest is usually told that the room in question has no current occupant.

- Two hotel guests from Atlanta reported, "When we checked into here, we discovered that every drawer in our room was open. Two nightstands, a chest of drawers, every single one. We called the desk clerk about this, and he assured us that housekeeping would have never left the room like that." They dismissed the matter, closed the drawers and went out to dinner. Upon their return later that night, they were surprised when they opened the door to the room and found that again all of the drawers and cupboard doors were wide open. They called down to the desk to inquire why housekeeping had come into their room and done this again but were assured that housekeeping had all left for the day. According to the guests, upon learning this, "We asked for a different room!"

- Many guests report hearing footsteps and finding doors, drawers and curtains opened or closed.
- Several employees and guests have gotten images in the backgrounds of photographs that appear to contain faces; this happens most often when a mirror or other reflective surface is in the background.
- Several paranormal groups have conducted investigations of the Admiral Fell Inn. There is considerable agreement about existence of paranormal activities in the building, but no one has ever been able to attach a specific personality or individual to most of the activities.
- Investigators from the television show *Ghost Detectives* conducted several days of on-site investigation in 2012 and received a number of extraordinary electromagnetic readings/signatures, as well as several fascinating thermal images. One significant reading was located on a bed in a room where a manager had once seen a "white glow" hovering over the mattress. Check out the Ghost Detectives website to see video of the investigation: www.ghostdetectives.tv.

Rye Craft Cocktails (formerly Leadbetters Tavern)

1639 Thames Street

The building occupied by Rye (Leadbetters Tavern until 2016) was originally a mid-nineteenth-century shop with some upstairs living space; quite often, these rooms were occupied by seamen and other temporary lodgers. Many of the buildings near the harbor operated as informal boardinghouses and taverns until the early twentieth century and—during Prohibition years—as speak-easies or flophouses. The alley at the back of

1639 Thames allowed for discreet entrances (as well as quick escapes from police raids), and after Prohibition came to an end the building housed a succession of taverns.

In the late twentieth century, the tavern was called Leadbetters, and the owners needed to expand the first floor in order to accommodate a women's restroom. They took out one of the back walls and extended the building into the alley space that lay behind it, installed plumbing and fixtures and put a large mirror over the sink. And then strange things began to happen.

Guests and employees washing up at the sink of an empty restroom began rushing out of the new bathroom—sometimes hysterical—because they had seen a man standing behind them when they looked into the mirror. They described his long, unkempt brown hair and his worn and tattered clothing and shivered as they remembered the look of despair and sadness on his face. Many of them said that one of his white hands had reached out, as if to stroke their hair or touch their shoulder. Her heart pounding, each woman had spun quickly to face the intruder—only to discover that no one stood behind them.

During the 1870s, the body of a man was discovered in the back alley that later became part of the new bathroom. His trousers, kerchief and jacket made it obvious that he was a sailor, but he was never identified and later buried in an anonymous grave. It was not difficult to figure out how he died—the back of his skull had been crushed by a heavy blow—but opinions differed on what had happened. Some thought the man had been targeted by crimpers while he was drinking in the tavern or that a press gang had dragged him into the alley and used a cosh with a little too much enthusiasm. Others pointed to the fact that he had been stripped of any valuables and believed the cause was a violent mugging. Whether he was the target of a press gang or the victim of a robbery will never be known, but however he met his end, this mysterious sailor is not ready to set sail for a new destination, and sightings continue into the present day.

The building is also haunted by the malevolent spirit of a violent man, a cruel and abusive husband and father who was killed by his own son on one horrible night in the 1960s. The family lived in an apartment on the second floor, an address local police were unpleasantly familiar with; neighbors had called in complaints on more than one occasion, reporting screams and even gunshots. The wife was obviously terrified of her husband, but there was little social support for abused women, and she had nowhere to go. Without her husband's paycheck, she and her children would fall into dire poverty and desperation. But one night, an already dangerous situation grew worse;

after returning home from a drinking binge, the man began to beat his wife so viciously that she thought he was going to kill her. The children cowered in a corner, desperate with fear, and at some point, their father turned away from beating their mother and advanced toward them, flexing his fingers and shouting threats. Terrified, one of his sons took up his father's gun and shot him in the head, killing him instantly. When police arrived, they found a horrible scene.

The boy was taken into custody and sent to a mental institution for evaluation; on determining that he had acted in self-defense, no charges were filed, and he was released from the hospital to return to his family.

Many years later, a young man entered the building, which was then occupied by Leadbetters Tavern. Taking a seat at the bar, he ordered a beer and asked to speak to the manager. When Donna arrived, he introduced himself and explained that he had been that boy, and he had never returned to the apartment upstairs since the night he shot his father. He wanted to visit the apartment to see if he could find some way to close a door on that portion of his past and asked for the key. Donna gave him permission, handed him her key and watched him walk up the stairs. But before the man reached the top step, he turned, walked back downstairs to the bar and sat on his barstool, sipping at his beer and seemingly conducting an inaudible conversation with an invisible companion. He had his head turned to the side, as if listening intently, and he nodded and murmured occasional

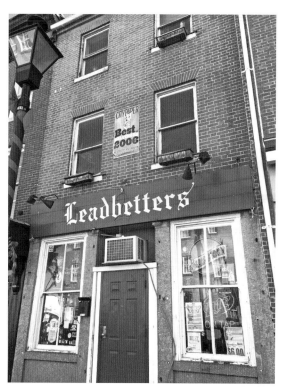

The second floor of the former Leadbetters Tavern (now Rye Craft Cocktails) once housed the family of a violent alcoholic; he died at the hands of his son. *Author photo.*

responses. After a while, he straightened up, asked Donna for the check and left a generous tip along with the unused key to the apartment he had been so desperate to visit. She was convinced that the young man succeeded in finding the closure he wanted because he never returned. "It was odd," another manager remembered, "the one who caused the ghost came in and wanted to talk to him."

This ghost is also blamed for angry outbursts in and around the bar. Liquor bottles are knocked from shelves, drinks spilled on the bar, heavy footsteps go up and down the stairs and a second-floor door—always kept locked—will slam open and shut. The presence of this spirit is associated with a sense of menace and barely suppressed anger, manifested in cruel jokes and occasionally dangerous situations. Heavy objects have fallen from shelves, missing people by inches; ice cubes are strewn across tile floors as if to encourage a fall; and chairs are pulled out from beneath people as they sit. A former manager, who once lived in the second-floor apartment, said, "I swear I've seen him and felt him walking around up there. The sucker knocked on my door three or four times a week, at 4:00 a.m."

In one particularly frightening case, it was manager Donna who was the target of a violent and unexplained attack, which took place as she was closing down for the night.

All of the other staff had left for the evening, and Donna had been careful to be sure that all of the doors were locked before she began counting out the cash drawers and preparing the bank deposit. Once everything was safely locked in the safe, she turned out the office lights and walked out into the bar, intending to turn out the lights and head home. She heard no sound and had seen no one in the bar, but she was grabbed by the throat and thrown to the ground; she felt a blow to her head, and everything went black. When Donna awoke, several hours had passed, and she was lying in a pool of blood on the floor of the bar. She managed to pull her cellphone from her purse and call the owner of the bar, who lived in the upstairs apartment. When he arrived, he immediately called for an ambulance and the police.

Even though the doors were still locked and bolted (the owner needed a key to get inside), it appeared that Donna had been assaulted during the course of a robbery. But it seemed that nothing had been taken—and all of the doors were secured and locked from the inside. A medical examination by the paramedics found bruising around Donna's neck, as if she'd been taken in a chokehold, and the blow to her head had not come from striking the floor but from being hit with a heavy object. The injuries were so severe that she spent several days in the hospital ICU. Despite a careful search, police were unable to discover any evidence of an intruder.

The staff has tried many different methods in their efforts to pacify the aggressive spirit—and some of them appear to have some effect. After hearing that ghosts like peppermint candy (an old wives' tale), they put a jar of peppermints high up on a shelf, hoping to steer the ghost away from the staff and patrons. The mints began disappearing one by one, and to this day the jar needs to be refilled every couple months. Another ploy was to leave a shot of whiskey on a shelf before closing up for the night; the first time they tried it, the glass was empty the next morning—and some of the banging and slamming stopped. Since that time, the bartender will leave a shot of whiskey out about once a month—and the glass is always empty in the morning.

Perhaps Donna's attack was the act of a man who felt no qualms about attacking a defenseless woman, or it could be that she was "coshed" by a crimper. Or it could be that there are even more unquiet and dangerous spirits adrift in this building, their names and motivations unknown.

3

THE DANGEROUS BUSINESS OF SEX

Remove prostitutes from human societies and you will throw everything into confusion through lusts.
—*St. Augustine,* De Ordine, *2.12*

Under the name of the Great Social Evil our newspapers for years have alluded to an awful vice, too evidently of wide prevalence [prostitution]...
—*Francis William Newman, in an 1869 religious tract*

We point out the location of these places in order that the reader may know how to avoid them, and that he may not select one of them for his boarding house when he comes to the city.
—The Gentleman's Directory, *a guide to the brothels of New York, published in 1870*

For much of human history, prostitution has been a fact of life. In early times, prostitutes were often associated with certain deities, such as the Babylonian Ishtar and Greek Aphrodite, and may have practiced their profession within temple walls (although it is more likely that they simply paid a tax to religious authorities). Even after Christianity engulfed most of Europe, prostitution continued—regarded by the Roman Catholic Church as a "necessary evil" because it provided income to desperate women and offered a "release" for men's natural lusts.

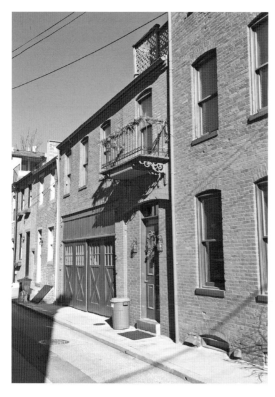

Although it looks respectable now, this house on Shakespeare Street near South Bethel was once occupied by a brothel. *Author photo.*

Prostitution was generally condemned on moral grounds by the middle class, which tends to be socially conservative, but the wealthy were more accepting (many powerful men publicly supported a mistress) and the poor tended to treat working prostitutes as fellow citizens. For much of Western history, civil authorities largely ignored prostitutes as long as they made no disturbances, and brothels could be found in nearly every neighborhood—including the wealthiest.

In the United States, the presence of the world's "oldest profession" can be traced back to the earliest settlements in Virginia and New England, and Fells Point was no different than any other port town—the brothels of the Point were a by-word among sailors and travelers. The "Captain's Hotel," now owned by the Preservation Society of Fells Point, was described by one nineteenth-century sailor as "the finest brothel in a town of many fine brothels." The names, addresses and attributes of such houses were passed around (and even published in private "gentleman's" directories).

There were "respectable houses" that catered to the wealthy—filled with expensive furniture, European art, French wines and sophisticated (and often well-educated) ladies; for merchants and the middle-class, comfortable houses staffed with local talent; and for the working man, there were the many taverns, most of which held a warren of tiny rooms and a variety of female entrepreneurs.

Prostitutes who worked off the streets were lowest on the social scale; they earned the least and worked out of dark alleys or shared a shabby room

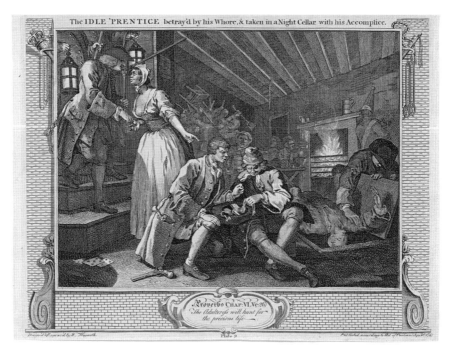

The IDLE 'PRENTICE betray'd by his Whore, & taken in a Night Cellar with his Accomplice.

Proverbs Chap. VI. Ve. 26.
The Adulteress will hunt for
the precious life.

A prostitute betrays her customers to their employer. As societal attitudes changed, working-class prostitutes were often portrayed as morally bankrupt. *New York Public Library.*

with other women. A woman working on her own was a target for rape, kidnapping, robbery and murder, so many prostitutes worked in partnership with a man—either willingly or unwillingly—in order to have some measure of protection. Many of these partnerships involved other crimes—vulnerable customers could be robbed or drugged and sold to a sea captain needing to fill out his crew.

Baltimore's criminal code didn't treat prostitution as a crime until the late nineteenth century. Up until that point, brothels and rooming houses were not generally targeted by legal authorities unless neighbors issued a complaint about rowdy behavior or noise—in fact, prostitutes could (and did!) file civil suits against neighborhood moral vigilantes who destroyed their property or interfered with their ability to do business.[13]

But the business of sex was supposed to be discreet—any prostitute (any unaccompanied woman, actually) could be accused of "night-walking," a holdover from English common law that meant that the accused had appeared in public at the wrong time, in the wrong place, while poor and female.

Over the course of the nineteenth century, attitudes toward prostitution began to change. Christian activists and social reformers saw it as a "great social evil," one that reduced both men and women to the lowest levels of moral degradation. In the name of "decency," laws were changed, and criminal (as well as civil) charges could be filed against prostitutes and customers. This shift in thinking meant that the brothels of Fells Point were forced to pay bribes to remain in business; customer traffic didn't diminish, but profits did, and the women who worked in the brothels were now subject to intimidation and blackmail.[14]

Once the crackdown really got going, brothel owners were forced to new levels of discretion. Because many visitors to Fells Point were illiterate or did not speak English, the names of taverns had always been illustrated by a sign above the door—a depiction of a red lion or gray gull, for example. Because of the fogs and mists that plagued the harbor area, many establishments also had oil lamps, gas lights and, later, electric bulbs, set behind colored panes; and lights like these were often used to identify brothels. A visiting sailor would ask where he could find companionship for the evening and would be told to look for the "Four Red Lamps" on Thames Street or the "Blue Lantern" on Elliott.[15] In 1888, the Port Mission, a Christian social outreach group, compiled a map of the Point that identified 323 saloons and 113 "houses of ill repute"—which definitely makes the Fells Point neighborhood a "red light district."*

While the demand for sex was the underlying reason for the existence of brothels, a surprising amount of nonsexual activity took place between customers and prostitutes. There are written accounts of brothel visits in nineteenth-century Fells Point in which the entire evening was spent in the parlor as a group, drinking and talking about the news and gossip of the day—racking up a big bar bill—but leaving without going upstairs. Customers had "special" girls that they enjoyed visiting, and marriages were not infrequent.[16]

For freedmen and, later, the post–Civil War African American working class, brothels were social spaces that allowed them to relax. Singer Billie Holiday ran errands and did odd jobs for Alice Dean, who ran a brothel on the corner near Billie's home on South Durham Street. It was the only brothel

---

* At the dawn of the twentieth century, American brothels were most often located in a city's "red light district." Such areas tended to have transient populations and poorer inhabitants, and municipal authorities usually turned a blind eye to prostitution, so long as the appropriate bribes were paid. The origin of this term is a matter of debate, with some claiming that it comes from the practice of railroad engineers, who, while patronizing a brothel, would hang their red-paned signaling lanterns outside the door. Others point to the fact that brothels often used pink or red lamps in their interior rooms. There is also a theory that the term arose as a comparison between the brightly colored lights of an adult entertainment district and the street lighting in hell—a harbinger of the fires of perdition to come!

in Fells Point that had a record player, and it was there that the young girl first listened to Louis Armstrong and Bessie Smith.

But life in even the best brothel was not free of danger; prostitutes were at the mercy of the owner, as well as the customers, who were frequently drunk and violent. Many women were maimed or killed by customers, brothel owners and, in one famous Baltimore case, a husband![17]

And it's easy to forget that simply having sex could be lethal.

With no reliable method of birth control until the late twentieth century, few prostitutes escaped becoming pregnant. A woman could die from a botched abortion. If she went through with the pregnancy, there was a good chance she could die in childbirth. If mother and baby survived the birth, either could die of infection in the days that followed.

Sexually transmitted diseases were another danger—gonorrhea and syphilis were common and incurable. If the infection became obvious, a prostitute's career went into a literal death spiral; she died of the disease or of the poverty, violence and homelessness that were the inevitable results. Other illnesses got passed along as well; getting up close and personal with a man infected with influenza, smallpox, yellow fever, typhoid, measles or mumps was a sure way to contract the same illness. There were a thousand ways for a prostitute to die before thirty, and many of them did—especially those working the streets.

Modern ideas about sex work and prostitution lead many to believe that the prostitutes of the past were forced into the life, but this does not seem to be the case. While some women were undoubtedly coerced, others saw it as a better alternative to poverty or scraping by on the meager salary of a factory worker. During the nineteenth century, social reformers in New York conducted interviews with prostitutes and were shocked to discover that a majority of them did not wish to work at a "respectable" job—they were perfectly happy making three or four times as much in far less respectable positions.

Undoubtedly, some of the prostitutes in Fells Point's history would have chosen to live a different life, but it is also quite likely that many of them would have chosen no other. While there were many dangers, there were also benefits: better pay, safer housing and the possibility of marriage or a discreet partnership with a wealthy patron.

And quite a few of these ladies have chosen to remain in the buildings where they once practiced their profession, and they are constantly getting up to new tricks.

CAT'S EYE PUB

1730 Thames Street

True story from Julia Dray: On my first visit to the Cat's Eye—probably around 1990—I walked up the uneven brick steps, opened the door, stepped into the bar and was forced to stop in my tracks because there were two bodies on the floor—a man and a woman, completely motionless and locked in each other's arms. After a moment, I realized that the entwined limbs could meant that they were either (*A*) having the most intense kiss EVER, (*B*) were unconscious from too much alcohol or (*C*) were dead.

I froze for a moment but then realized that there were people at the bar, and none of them were panicking. No one seemed to understand why I had stopped moving toward the bar; they all looked at me with a certain amount of confusion. I plastered on a confident smile and stepped over the recumbent figures—although I did look down to see if they were breathing. Other customers followed me in, and I was amazed at the lack of concern they displayed—barely breaking stride as they stepped over the pair, who remained locked in a motionless embrace. But twenty minutes later, when the two of them sleepily staggered back to their feet and left, I was involved in a deep discussion about crossword puzzles with the bartender and could barely be bothered to notice. The Cat's Eye is just that sort of place.

One of the unique features of this bar is the "Wall of Death,"

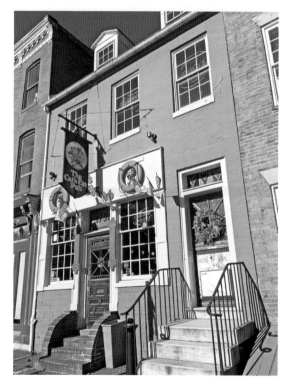

The Cat's Eye Pub on Thames Street. The door at right once opened onto a staircase that gave access to the brothel upstairs. *Author photo.*

a photographic display of deceased employees, regular customers and owners. The pub has always celebrated its neighborhood clientele; seldom fashionable, but always defiantly itself, the pub continues the Fells Point tradition of democratic hospitality combined with just the right amount of Baltimore sass, sex and snark.

The building that houses the Cat's Eye Pub was built in the early to mid-nineteenth century; the two-story row house was originally a shop with upstairs living quarters that had a separate entrance to the street. The building might have originally housed some innocent or innocuous business, but because of its proximity to the waterfront it was a prime site for a tavern. By the time of the American Civil War, the main floor held a long bar and many small tables; the second floor consisted of a warren of small rooms, which were accessible through a separate street entrance and a very narrow staircase leading up from the barroom.

The upper floors belonged to the ladies, who were each given a room with basic furnishings that they were encouraged to decorate themselves. Some chose lace and flowery prints, while others chose to hang flowing draperies

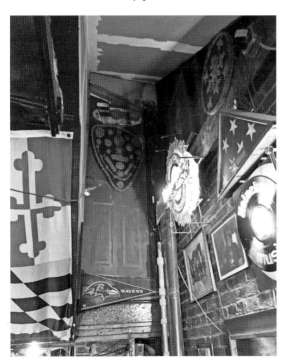

from the ceiling to mimic tents or covered the walls with cheap wallpaper decorated with naughty scenes. Every woman tried to find a niche that distinguished her from the competition—wearing lingerie and French perfume, for example, providing a certain kind of atmosphere in her room or catering to certain fetishes.

In exchange for her room and board, and possibly even her clothing, every woman paid a percentage of her earnings to the house. In order to keep an eye on the flow of customers, entrance

Although the staircase was removed long ago, the upstairs door to the brothel still remains. *Author photo.*

to the upper floors was generally restricted by a gatekeeper, usually a large gentleman with a cudgel, who not only counted the number of customers but also prevented drunken or jealous men from forcing their way upstairs. At the Cat's Eye, the separate street entrance that led to the upper floors would most likely have been kept locked, and customers would only be able to enter from within the bar.

The bar itself—high-ceilinged, long and narrow—had rough wooden floors and a reputation for catering to a shady clientele. The network of narrow alleys that were accessible from the back entrance made it a perfect rendezvous point for criminal fences during peacetime, Confederate sympathizers during the American Civil War and war profiteers during every conflict.

During the Civil War, many brothel owners used their prostitutes to gather information for either the Union or the Confederacy, but in this building, the owner evidently had no political agenda—he liked everybody's money, and the war was good to him. But the times were about to get harder.

By the late nineteenth century, much of the shipping industry that had sustained the Point had relocated; runoff from the city and catastrophic flooding had filled the harbor with silt. Small boats and barges still tied up at the wharves on Thames Street, sending cargoes of produce or oysters to the canneries, but commerce gradually moved away—into downtown Baltimore or east to the new shipyards on Locust and Sparrows Point. The stately houses of the merchant class were subdivided into apartments, the large business buildings became rooming houses and empty warehouses were filled by machinists' workshops and small factories. Expensively appointed brothels like the Merchant's Hotel closed their doors, and the population grew poorer and more transient.

But the waterfront is never still, even when the traffic has turned into fishing boats and barges filled with carrots, and the inexpensive housing in Fells Point attracted new immigrants, many of them single men. (Between the Civil War and World War I, more than two million immigrants arrived in Baltimore.) The Cat's Eye remained a center for shady activities, and the ladies upstairs were a prime attraction.

During the years of Prohibition (1920–33), the taverns of Fells Point stayed open, although they operated a little more discreetly. Neither the State of Maryland nor the City of Baltimore spent much time enforcing federal Prohibition laws—all it took to stay out of trouble was a low profile and substantial bribes.

When Prohibition ended, the illicitly funded prosperity of Fells Points' bars and clubs also came to an end, and the neighborhood slid further into decay. By the 1960s, the building was nearly derelict, but it was substantially renovated in the 1970s and named the Cat's Eye Pub.

The building is said to be haunted by a number of spirits, from former prostitutes to previous owners, and reports of activity are common—most of the regular customers and nearly all of the staff have at least one story of something strange that happened to them at the Cat's Eye.

One of the most frequent occurrences are the loud, mechanical clicks that seem come from behind the wall between the bar and the front windows; these sounds are followed by the echo of footsteps, which retreat to the back of the building.

The potential source of the noises is hidden behind the wallboard between the bar and the front windows: a bank of switches that once controlled the exterior and interior lighting in the building. Originally installed in the 1890s, the switches were operated by turning a metal "key" that latched into place—each key turned power on or off for specific sets of lights.

There is a popular story in Fells Point that claims that these switches controlled lights that showed which ladies were "free" at a given time. While this theory has the virtue of being risqué, it is probably completely false; nothing like that was a recorded practice at any Baltimore-area brothel.

It is important to remember that the "ladies" were entertainers as much as sexual partners; they sang and danced in the bar, chatted with gentlemen and mingled with the crowd, where they might catch the eye of a wealthy

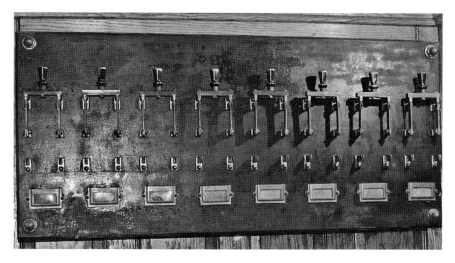

During a renovation, antique switches like these were discovered behind a wall. Patrons hear the distinctive clicking sound of the switches being turned on and off. *Author photo.*

or generous patron or earn money by partnering customers in dances or by encouraging them to spend money at the bar. Working girls didn't wait upstairs for a random client; they did their best to pick the best customer in the establishment.

Instead, the switches were probably handled by whomever opened and closed the tavern; some were exterior lights, but others activated incandescent bulbs in the bar and upstairs hallways and stairwells. (The individual bedrooms were probably lit as well but could also have used gas fixtures.) The lights would have been turned on when it began to grow dark and turned off at close of business—which would account for the timing of the phenomena.

Beneath the layer of drywall, the lights of long ago are being turned on—and off. Rather a suitable description of a brothel haunting, isn't it?

But the ghosts of the Cat's Eye are a varied lot—while there are a lot of women who still enjoy spending their evenings in the bar (or above it), there are also stories that show that loose women aren't the only spirits in the place…there are a couple of men on the loose, as well.

- One young man had an unsettling encounter with a pretty girl, who walked past his group as they stood in the back room. He admired her walk and the way it made the long skirts of her low-necked vintage dress sway over the low-heeled red shoes on her tiny feet; he smiled at her when she caught his eye. She returned the smile and held his gaze as she walked past the table and out the back door, which stood open to the night air. "I thought she was some RennFaire chick," he explained. "As soon as she went out the door, I said something to the guys with me, but none of them had noticed her. Literally a second later, two of my buddies came in from the back—they'd been standing right outside the door, kind of blocking it, and they said they hadn't seen her either. 'There wasn't anybody else out there, man.' So I went and looked—and it was only like a minute later—and she wasn't there."

- In several of the rooms on the second floor, furnishings mysteriously appear and disappear. One bartender once opened a door and saw a room that was completely draped in fabric that shrouded a large bed and smelled of incense. He heard a throaty female laugh, and the door slammed shut; when he managed to wrest it open again, the room had returned to its normal state. Another report describes a painting that appeared on a wall along the second-floor hallway; it depicted a waterfront scene and was framed in a carved frame whose gilding was cracked and flaking. The visitor who saw the painting asked one of the employees about it, only to receive a puzzled look in reply; the visitor insisted on going back upstairs to look, and the employee went with him. There was nothing on the wall except a hole that had been patched long ago.

- Some witnesses report hearing the sound of light footsteps clicking across the wooden floors or throaty female laughter from behind the bar; others claim to have seen women in low-cut and ruffled costumes looking from the upper windows or standing on the steps outside the doors.

- On the floors that held the brothel chambers, doors open and close, clocks are set backward or forward and lights and small appliances turn on and off. The voices of both men and women laugh, whisper and shout; shadowy figures hover at the corners of the eyes, and sudden cold spots send ice into the bones.

- The building is also said to be haunted by the spirit of Kenny Orye, the former owner and harmonica enthusiast, whose photograph is displayed on the "Wall of Death." (Orye died

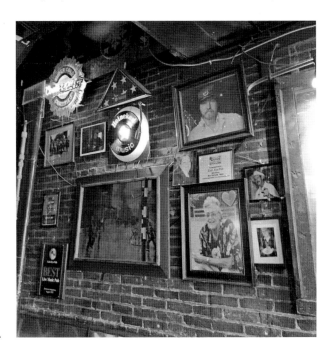

The "Wall of Death" at the Cat's Eye showcases the photographs of deceased employees and customers. Former owner Kenny Orye and bartender Jeff Knapp are both said to haunt the building. *Author photo.*

in December 1987.) Several bartenders have reported hearing someone playing the harmonica, and on one occasion, an antique harmonica mysteriously appeared behind the bar. Buckets fly off of shelves, bottles and glasses slide and fall and Kenny's photograph has—on at least one occasion—fallen off the wall and landed directly on the head of someone who was reminiscing about him in a negative fashion.

- Longtime bartender Jeff Knapp, who died of a heart attack in 1992 at the age of sixty-three, was a dead ringer for Abraham Lincoln and a genuine local character. He once created a cemetery for dolls in the courtyard behind the pub, where, according to the *Baltimore Sun*, "Ken and Barbie were buried after a suicide pact, GI Joe succumbed to Agent Orange and a cole slaw shredder was on hand for deceased Cabbage Patch dolls." In the years since his death, several people have mentioned the bartender who looks like Abraham Lincoln and their recent interaction with him—the pouring of a beer or the purchase of a shirt. When his photo on the Wall of Death is pointed out to them, they have all positively identified him as the bartender they were talking about, only to be dumbfounded to discover that he passed on a decade before.

Whether attracted to the spirits of long-gone girls or merely attracted to spirits, customers run the risk of being turned on at the Cat's Eye.

MERCHANTS HOUSE AND THE HORSE TROLLEY BARN: THE FELLS POINT VISITORS CENTER

1724–26 Thames Street

The Merchants House (or Hotel), a building that now contains the Fells Point Visitors Center, dates from around 1800 and operated as a saloon and brothel while also offering cheap rooms for visiting merchants and sailors. The building was an unsavory place to stay—as with most of the dodgy rooming houses of Fells Point, the unwary sailor faced serious dangers when he checked in. Many of the paranormal events reported fit the description of stuff that happens when men drink too much and there are scantily clad women running around: sultry whispers, unsteady footsteps thudding through the halls and on the stairs, loud and incoherent arguments, a woman screaming, the sound of doors slamming and quiet sobbing.

In a 2012 incident, a police officer responded to the report of an attempted break-in at the building during the late hours of the night. He was conducting a room-by-room search when he entered an upstairs room that contained nothing but an empty bed frame…that was moving. The officer swore that it looked as if somebody was jumping up and down on it, and he was so terrified that he bolted out of the building, called for backup and flatly refused to re-enter that room. Given the history of the building, the ghost is probably not "jumping" on the bed, but it's not impossible.

The adjoining Horse Trolley Barn, at 1726 Thames Street, also owned by the Fells Point Preservation Society, operated as a horse trolley barn from the late eighteenth century until the advent of street rail in the late nineteenth and is also said to be haunted. The building was used for a variety of commercial purposes in the twentieth century, and no one knows who could be haunting it or why. Just listen for the footsteps that pace back and forth on the main floor and keep an eye out for the shadowy figure of a man who stands in a corner near one of the Thames Street doorways.

STICKY RICE (FORMERLY FRIENDS BAR)

1634 Aliceanna Street

The building at 1634 Aliceanna Street was used as a brothel at various points in its history, and it is said to be haunted by the spirits of former working girls who are evidently still enthusiastic about their profession. Paranormal activity has occurred on the ground floor, as well as in the rooms above; objects moving, doors opening, the sounds of female voices and footsteps and high EMF readings have all been reported.

The apartment above the bar has been rented by a number of people, and many have experienced at least one unsettling experience while living in its rooms. One tenant reported being awakened one night by the loud cries and moans of a woman in the throes of passion, and another described waking late one night because his bed was moving "violently back and forth, up and down."

THE CAPTAIN'S HOTEL

1629–31 Aliceanna Street

The two three-story row homes at this address are covered in formstone, the faux-stone façade that was used in Baltimore throughout the twentieth century. With the original brick façade completely covered, the buildings look far more contemporary than they are, but they date from the first years of the nineteenth century and once contained one of Baltimore's most famous brothels, the "Captain's Hotel."

This high-class, exclusive establishment had a heavy carved wood bar on the first floor and thickly carpeted hallways and stairs that led to a warren of small rooms on the upper stories, where the "ladies" could entertainment gentlemen in private. There have been a number of reports of paranormal phenomena in the buildings: the sound of footsteps along the halls and on the stairs, moving objects and doors that slam without a breath of wind to blame.

The buildings are currently owned by the Fells Point Preservation Society, which also owns the green-painted wooden building to one side. Built in 1797, this building housed Nicholas Leakey's Academy during the early nineteenth century. Keep an eye out for a teenage boy in a white shirt and dark knee breeches pacing in front of 1627 Aliceanna; whether he is waiting for his next class at the academy or working up his courage to try the door of the Captain's Hotel will never be known.

4

A Chariot of Death

YELLOW FEVER IN BALTIMORE

The disease, rising from the rank of a bilious [fever], to that of a yellow fever, mounted its chariot of death, and spread dismay and mourning wherever it appeared.
—*Moreau de Saint Me'ry, French refugee from Haiti, 1793*

In 1793, Maryland was no stranger to epidemics; malaria (called "intermittent fever"), scarlet fever, cholera, measles, smallpox and influenza all swept through at intervals, sickening many, but were usually fatal only to the very young or very old—smallpox being an exception.[18] But when yellow fever arrived, this devastating illness didn't play by those rules.

It was commonly accepted that dangerous fevers came from breathing bad air—noxious vapors rose from stagnant water during the summer months—and the wind carried pestilence into towns. To escape, wealthy families left for the country from July to September, retreating to cooler and higher-altitude summer properties. Working-class people had no choice but to remain in the humid environs of Fells Point, a pragmatic choice that turned deadly in 1793, when yellow fever came to Baltimore.

We now know that proximity to water was a key reason for the spread of the disease, but noxious gases had nothing to do with it. Instead, clouds of *Aedes aegypti* mosquitoes swarmed out of the shallow coastal swamps and went into town for dinner. After sipping blood from an infected sailor (the most likely disease vector), a female mosquito only had to survive for two weeks—at which point, her next bite could infect a new victim. Eggs laid by an infected mosquito could carry the virus, and an infected larva that survived to adulthood spread yellow fever with every bite.

Many historians believe that it was French emigrants—driven out of Haiti by the slave revolution in 1793—who brought the infection to Baltimore. The epidemic started in July 1793 in Fells Point, but the outbreak spread up the Chesapeake Bay as far north as Philadelphia. In total, the epidemic claimed more than twenty-five thousand lives on the Eastern Seaboard of the United States, a total that sounds paltry to modern ears, but which accounted for nearly one in twelve residents.[19]

It was a cruel sickness—victims appeared to recover after two days of high fever, vomiting and aches, only to relapse and suffer from spontaneous bleeding, shock, kidney failure and severe jaundice of the liver, which led to yellowing of the skin and the whites of the eyes (hence, "yellow" fever).[20]

A physician present in Fells Point during the 1793 epidemic, Dr. Nathaniel Potter, claimed that half the inhabitants of the Point were "dead or fled" and that he'd seen evidence of bodies being clandestinely and illegally buried by night. The epidemic subsided as the weather grew cooler, and by November, the number of new cases had slowed to a trickle.

The majority of the deaths in Baltimore occurred in Fells Point, where several thousand were infected and many died. (The epidemic contributed to the flight of the merchant class from the neighborhood in the ensuing years.) There weren't many hospitals—people were nursed at home—and not all deaths were reported to authorities. Figures vary from account to account, but it seems likely that 700 to 1,000 people died in Fells Point and at least 345 in Baltimore town. Fells Point remained an epicenter for infections into early twentieth century; it was one of the neighborhoods hardest hit by the influenza pandemic that followed World War I.

Many Fells Point storytellers and tours describe the presence of a mass grave said to be located in the heart of Fells Point, claiming that thousands of victims of yellow fever lie beneath the streets. There is absolutely no evidence to substantiate this claim.[21]

There were between seven hundred and one thousand fatalities in Fells Point over a four-month period, and while that might mean that gravediggers were working overtime, there are still legible gravestones in local cemeteries of people who died in the epidemic. Most surviving church registers hold multiple entries for burials of yellow fever victims in their cemeteries. There are several contemporaneous accounts that describe two or three bodies being illicitly buried in parks or vacant lots, but these burials were carried out by individuals—possibly boardinghouse owners or the very poor—and would have been in scattered locations.

While there is no mass grave of yellow fever victims, there are definitely bodies buried beneath the streets and alleys of Fells Point, victims of violence or accident, whose remains were hidden from sight only to be discovered as re-development and reconstruction slowly excavate the past.

BERTHA'S MUSSELS

734 South Broadway

Bertha's Mussels opened in 1972 and was one of the first sit-down restaurants in Fells Point. The business encompasses three interconnected buildings that date to 1790–1820 and variously enjoyed careers as homes, brothels, taverns and shops in the past two centuries. Paranormal activity is so frequent (and so disturbing) that employees were once reportedly required to sign a waiver acknowledging that Bertha's would not pay for therapy as a result of anything that they might see or hear on the property.

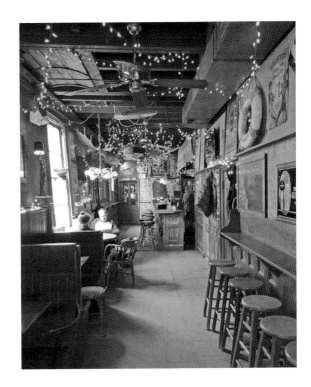

The bar at Bertha's, where mysterious customers hang out after staff have gone home. *Author photo.*

Quite a few paranormal investigators have visited the restaurant, and while they have gotten very active EMF and EVP (Electronic Voice Phenomena) readings, few have managed to capture a recording of any of the men and women or the little girl that have been spotted over the years. Most of the existing video was captured by Bertha's security cameras, which survey all of the public and private areas in the restaurant.

The ghosts in the building come from many eras. Several are said to be unfortunate victims of the 1793–94 yellow fever outbreak, while others perished in the 1918 influenza pandemic. Some ghosts wear the clothing of the mid-nineteenth and early twentieth centuries, while others are dressed in clothing from the early colonial years. The paranormal activity in the building has terrified so many employees that management warns every new hire, and everyone in the building knows that no one is to go up to the fourth floor alone. But several years ago, one of the restaurant's employees shrugged off the warnings and did just that. Unable to find someone to accompany him on a busy night, he went upstairs unaccompanied.

As he climbed the staircase, he was struck by a powerful feeling that he was not wanted—that he should turn and go back downstairs. Scoffing at himself for being superstitious, he continued to the landing at the top of the stairs and opened the door of the fourth-floor storage room.

Bright sunlight streamed through the windows and across the wooden planks of the floor, and he stared at the rocking chair and rusty bed that occupied a room that normally held ranks of storage shelves and kitchen equipment. A flicker of movement caught his eye, and he looked over into the corner to see a small girl playing at some game, her back to him. He made some noise, and she turned to look at him; he saw that within the frame of her hair, she had no face. Overcome with horror, he stumbled down the stairs and into the restaurant. "She didn't have a face!" was one of the things he screamed as he rushed out onto the streets. The man was so shaken that he never returned to work.

- Another man spotted a young girl dressed in mid-nineteenth-century attire, her long braids bouncing as she jumped rope on a second-floor landing. She has been tentatively identified as the daughter of a prostitute who worked in the building during the 1850s; the child is said to have died in a typhus epidemic in 1853.
- At least one psychic who has investigated the building has pointed to the closet of a second-floor room, claiming that the ghost of a

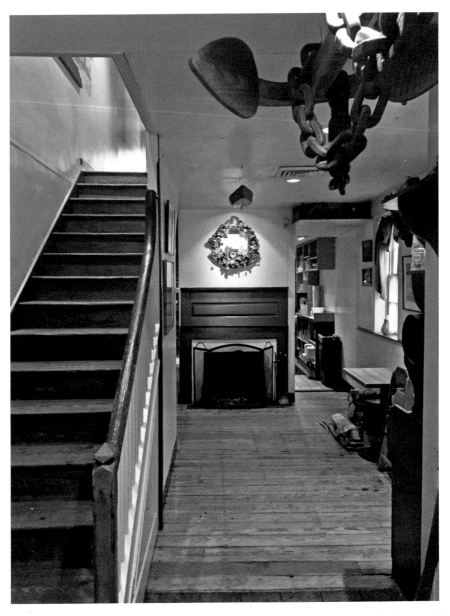

The second-floor landing of Bertha's has been the site of many encounters, including a young girl skipping rope. *Author photo.*

young girl is hiding inside it—perhaps having been forced to stay there when her mother had a customer. Whether or not this is the same ghost described earlier is unknown.

- Many people have spotted a pipe-smoking sailor in the dining room and reported items moving around on their tables; hair combs and pins have been plucked out and placed next to their drinks. Others report seeing faces in mirrors or reflected in glass; one woman glimpsed a man whose stringy hair hung about a narrow face that dripped with sweat and whose eyes stared into hers with a feverish intensity. Wracked by a sudden deep chill, the woman fell back against a wall; when she looked again, the face was gone.
- A bartender named Emily was closing up one night and walked through the dining room, carrying a tray of dirty glasses from the bar area back to the kitchen. She was shocked and surprised to see the figure of an old man, hazy and partially transparent, standing near the bread station, wearing a worn-out brown Derby hat and disheveled old clothes. She froze, and her jaw dropped. He looked at her, politely tipped his old hat with one hand and vanished. Completely terrified, Emily locked up and left in a hurry. On the following night, Emily was on duty with a woman who had worked at Bertha's for many years. Although nervous at mentioning what she'd witnessed, Emily felt the need to share the story with someone. She took a deep breath, told her story and was surprised to learn that others had seen the same man back in the dining room on many occasions.
- Evidence of the paranormal has also been detected by animals (visiting service dogs find the building unnerving), customer videos and photographs and the security system. Two men have appeared in the main bar on after-hours security footage several times: one is casually disposed on a bar stool, with his legs propped, while the other paces back and forth to the front door, for all the world as though he is waiting on a "late" companion.
- During one investigation, a large trunk on the second floor began rocking back and forth, and the image of a woman in black glided down the stairs leading from the restrooms, vanishing before she reached the hall below. Several paranormal investigators have worked on the site, and it is commonly used to train new ghost hunters in the use of their equipment.

5

No Town for Temperance

FELLS POINT DURING PROHIBITION

Prohibition is better than no liquor at all.
—*Will Rogers, American writer and humorist*

In Baltimore, the Prohibition movement began in 1840. In that year, six men, each struggling with issues related to alcohol, took a vow of abstinence in a Baltimore barroom. Members of what came to be called the "Baltimore Movement" didn't lobby to change liquor laws, and they didn't preach the evils of alcohol—it was a program that anticipated the modern "twelve-step" approach and stressed personal responsibility, supportive meetings and mentoring. It was an approach that failed to stem the tide of social decay and violence that accompanied Americans' thirst for alcohol.

The *Mayflower* carried more beer than fresh water on its voyage across the Atlantic, and the first major brewery in the colonies was opened by Dutch settlers in New Amsterdam (New York) in 1632. Wine, beer and distilled beverages were widely available, considered safer to consume than the local water, which was often contaminated. Every town in the colonies had at least one brewery, and the advent of cheap molasses from the Caribbean meant that rum distilleries sprang up alongside them in the 1700s.

Even Harvard College had a brewery; in 1639, when the school did not supply sufficient beer to the faculty and students, President Nathaniel Eaton lost his job. By the 1770s, the average adult male was consuming approximately three pints of eighty-proof every week—an amount that grew steadily because it cost less to get drunk with every year that passed. While habitual drunkards were social pariahs, a certain level of intoxication was common; by 1830, the average American adult consumed the equivalent of ninety bottles of eighty-proof liquor in every year, and one popular sheet-music title was "My Father Is a Drunkard and My Mother Is Dead."

Local, state and federal authorities attempted to stem the tide of cheap liquor, but the regulatory system was rife with corruption and taxes were evaded or simply not high enough. The fervor of the nationwide temperance movement was a reaction to the massive social cost of cheap and poorly regulated liquor.

Temperance advocates traveled the nation, addressing church congregations and political rallies. Many of the most fervent were women—some of whom believed in direct action—most famously Carrie Nation, who would invade saloons with an axe and stave in barrels of whiskey and beer. As the movement grew, elected officials were forced to declare themselves for or against the sale of alcohol, and by the turn of the twentieth century, a variety of forces were increasing the power of the movement. The Woman's Christian Temperance Union (WCTU), founded in 1873, had more than 200,000 members by 1920. The Anti-Saloon League, the WCTU and a host of other associations funded candidates in state and federal elections throughout the country, which paved the way for a proposal to amend the U.S. Constitution. The proposed amendment was sent to the state legislatures for ratification; in Maryland, Prohibition passed—to the amazement of everyone.

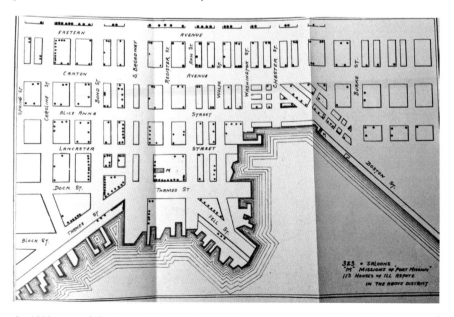

An 1880s map of the bars and brothels of Fells Point that was commissioned by the Women's Port Mission. *The Wharf Rat.*

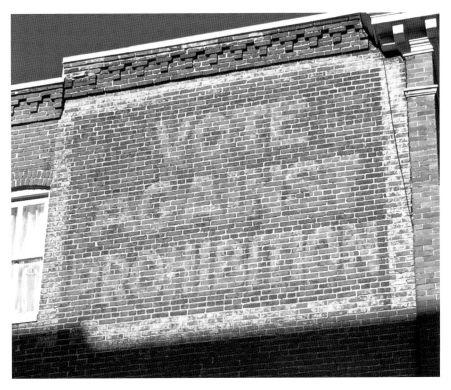

The idea of Prohibition was never popular in Fells Point, as this fading sign on the corner of Broadway and Shakespeare Street clearly demonstrates. *Author photo.*

On January 16, 1919, Nebraska became the thirty-sixth of the then forty-eight states to ratify the language of the Eighteenth Amendment to the U.S. Constitution, which banned the sale, transport and manufacture of liquor within the United States. In conjunction with the Volstead Act, which was passed by Congress in that same year (and outlined the spheres for state and federal action), the new amendment was initially hailed as an act of social progression but quickly proved to be the opposite. Selling illegal liquor made Al Capone rich, and it funded a thousand criminal enterprises and syndicates. (Even Capone once observed that "Prohibition has made nothing but trouble.")

The allure of the forbidden attracted young men and women to the "speak-easies," where they listened to modern music, danced scandalous dances and mingled with people of different social classes and races. Postwar and post–Spanish influenza America wanted to enjoy life—and that meant drinking. With the liquor laws poorly enforced and hardly prosecuted, the Eighteenth Amendment quickly came to be seen as a failure, but the political will to overturn it took thirteen years to develop.

From the beginning, the inhabitants of Fells Point wanted nothing to do with Prohibition. Modern visitors can glimpse their opinion in the faded paint on a brick wall at the corner of Shakespeare and Broadway: "Vote Against Prohibition." While the urban areas near Baltimore were overwhelmingly opposed, rural counties held a lot of "dry" voters. Prohibition activists packed the state's legislature with sympathetic politicians who steamrolled the vote for ratification. It was rushed through so quickly that the opposition never had a chance to stop it, and the governor signed it on February 13, 1918. Maryland's liquor lobby was blindsided, but it fought back and the "dry" majority was lost in the next election. Feisty Albert Ritchie, a notoriously "wet" politician, moved into the governor's mansion.

Governor Ritchie declined to enforce federal Prohibition laws, and Maryland never passed any state alcohol enforcement laws, so federal agents had to do it. The state government often declined to assist federal agents; in one case, when agents were roughed up in a tussle with bootleggers, the governor chided them for being unprepared. In another, Baltimore police looked the other way as a thirsty mob intercepted trucks full of confiscated beer, trapping the agents in the cabs and making off with most of the alcohol.[22]

In public obedience to the law, Baltimore's hoteliers and liquor wholesalers openly shipped their inventory out of town and off to the Bahamas, most frequently Nassau. From Nassau, the liquor was smuggled back into the city. For the next thirteen years, Nassau was at the epicenter of illegal liquor shipments, and the docks at Fells Point were a frequent destination.

Because of the complicity of nearly everyone in authority, Baltimore's liquor was not managed by organized crime, as in Chicago, Philadelphia or Boston. Liquor came into Baltimore from the surrounding countryside, where illegal stills pockmarked the western mountain valleys and the shallow creeks and waterways of the Eastern Shore. There was just no way to stop it—if you wanted to go out for a drink in Baltimore, you had quite a lot of choices.

Its convenient location on the wharves meant that Fells Point was filled with speak-easies, but due to lax enforcement, customers seldom needed to know a password. Bar owners paid bribes to police to ensure that they would be left alone. Some establishments were small, a side business for rooming houses and stores; others were large enough to allow dancing and space for small orchestras. Visitors to the Point also boarded ships for "cruises to nowhere"; once outside U.S. waters, the ships would cruise in circles until the alcohol ran out and it was time to return to port.

Like the rest of Baltimore's neighborhoods, Fells Point partied through the entire period of Prohibition and celebrated repeal without reservation.

It's not surprising that some die-hard partygoers have refused to leave—one of the most frequently reported paranormal events in the Admiral Fell Inn is the sound of drunken revelry in various hotel rooms.

RYE BAR (FORMERLY THE WHISTLING OYSTER)

807 South Broadway

In Matchett's Baltimore Directory of 1853–54, the property on Broadway between Lancaster Street and Thames Street was taken up by wharves, as was much of the area directly abutting the water. While a wharf is typically defined as a structure that extends onto the water, the term also encompasses the warehouses and piers associated with loading and unloading cargoes and could also refer to the commercial offices for each company using the docks, of which there were many.

The property probably held various businesses related to shipping until the late nineteenth century, but the buildings that now comprise 807–9 South Broadway were constructed on the site in 1920. The building at 807 was a speak-easy until Prohibition was repealed 1933, at which point a liquor license was legally obtained, and the property has been occupied by a bar ever since, usually with the owner or manager living in the apartment upstairs.

The speak-easy located here in the 1920s catered to those who worked in the canneries and factories of Fells Point. Where saloons and taverns catered exclusively to men and to women of a specific class (prostitutes), speak-easies were clubs that were patronized by both, and they marked the beginning of the cocktail age, where both sexes drank and socialized together. A piano provided much of the live music—Scott Joplin's ragtime pieces were hugely popular in Baltimore—but jazz groups often performed in the evenings.

After Prohibition was repealed, a succession of bars has occupied the premises, and many visitors and employees are convinced that the building is haunted by a variety of spirits. One frequently sighted apparition is a man who walks up a stairwell to the second floor—up stairs that were removed in a renovation of the building.

People hear ragtime music and laughter in the main bar area and catch fragments of whispered conversations and the sound of glasses clinking. The presence of a woman wearing a strong, musky perfume has been reported;

she is not seen, but felt—the gentle pressure of a hand on a shoulder, as she leans down to, perhaps, pick something up from the table. Customers will startle at the touch and turn, only to discover no one there.

One of the early residents on the site owned slaves, and some people believe that the ghost of an African American man, wearing colonial attire and carefully sweeping the floor near the fireplace, belongs to one of them.

One would expect that alcohol would be a big part of a haunting here, and it definitely is. Beer taps dispense beer at the touch of an unseen hand, bottles move out of position or fall on their sides and customers have reached for their drink at times, only to discover it sliding down the bar, as if pulled by an invisible string.

There is a number of stories about doors slamming and furniture moving about, and there is the usual collection of shadowy photographs and strange EVP recordings. No paranormal investigators have looked into the hauntings at the time of this writing, but one of the former owners/managers, who once lived above the business, swore that she could sense the presence of a ghost in the building. "It's definitely haunted, but it's just mischievous stuff," she told a reporter.

PROHIBITION TRIVIA

- Confident that alcohol was the cause of almost every criminal act, several towns actually sold their jails.
- A biblical scholar was hired by temperance activists to rewrite the Bible by removing any references to alcoholic beverages.
- Prohibitionists frequently pushed for extremely punitive measures for those who broke the law. Perhaps the most awful was the idea that the government itself would distribute poisonous alcohol to bootleggers, who would then disseminate it to the general population. When it was pointed out that several hundred thousand people would be killed by such a scheme, the proposers argued that it would be for the good of the nation. Among the more "humane" ideas put forward and seriously considered were exile to camps in the Aleutian Islands, banning marriage, branding, whipping, facial tattoos, placement in bottle-shaped cages in public squares, torture and sterilization.
- Because the bottles were too tall to be filled beneath the tap of a standard sink, it was necessary to use the bathtub spigot to dilute the

mixture of alcohol, glycerine and juniper juice that made "bathtub gin" so distinctive.

- The Speaker of the U.S. House of Representatives, Nicholas Longworth, owned and operated an illegal still.

- Some people believed that the undrinkable alcohol in antifreeze could be made safe by filtering it through a loaf of bread. It couldn't. Many people were blinded, suffered appalling injuries or died from drinking this "filtered" liquid.

- A Los Angeles jury that heard a bootlegging case faced criminal prosecution for drinking up the evidence. Although the jurors argued that they had simply been assuring themselves that the contents were alcoholic, the empty bottles meant that there was now no evidence against the bootlegger, who was acquitted.

- The modern ocean cruise was born during Prohibition because people could legally consume alcohol once the ship was in international waters. The ship would then cruise about in circles (hence the nickname "cruise to nowhere") until it was time to return to port.

- Prohibition was finally repealed at 4:31 p.m. on December 5, 1933, after lasting for thirteen years, ten months, nineteen days, seventeen hours and thirty-two and a half minutes; there are still hundreds of dry counties across the United States today.

6

THE ZEST OF SMUGGLING

*Forbid a man to think for himself or to act for himself and you may add the joy
of piracy and the zest of smuggling to his life.*
—Elbert Hubbard

The American Civil War brought an end to piracy on the Chesapeake
Bay; the Union navy's patrols made it impossible for marauding ships
and flotillas to operate. But pirates proved to be easier to eliminate than
other ship-borne lawbreakers; a canny smuggler avoids notice, relying on
stealth, camouflage and an intimate knowledge of the waterways and the
tides to conduct his business.

"Smuggling" is the act of importing goods to avoid the payment of
customs duties (taxes) or bringing unlawful products into a closed market
through stealth. Customs duties were (and are) imposed to protect domestic
industries from unfair competition, but they also bring revenue and offer a
method of controlling what enters an economy. There was (and is) a huge
incentive to smuggle goods under such conditions, and most fishermen
during the seventeenth and eighteenth centuries supplemented the profits of
their catch with a small inventory of illegal goods.

During the century that led up to the American Revolution, the
British government operated under an economic philosophy known as
"mercantilism," in which the colonies existed to enrich the mother country.
As a result, policies were enacted to control what goods colonists could
purchase, and the laws were written so that Americans had to buy British

goods from British merchants or pay expensive import duties. Merchants in Britain also had to pay duties on imported goods, such as tea, spices and silk.

Ships loaded with cargo subject to such taxes frequently chose to unload in isolated harbors or bribed customs inspectors and patrol vessels to look the other way. Until the 1760s, the British government was happy to look the other way, as this illicit trade enriched the merchants and trading companies. In the book *Smuggler Nation*, Peter Andreas writes, "Smuggling was so institutionalized in the Boston merchant community that merchants were able to buy insurance policies to cover them in the event of seizure."[23]

Because the cost of collecting customs duties was much greater than the amount of money they generated, Great Britain didn't make any special effort to control smuggling until the outbreak of the French and Indian War.[24] In an effort to limit the French profit from trade, goods purchased from French merchants in the French West Indies (or from Dutch, Spanish or Portuguese merchants) were interdicted; they became illegal under the Navigation and the Molasses Acts passed by Parliament.[25] Subsequent acts and tariffs followed.

American colonists were outraged at the restrictions to their trade and the greater costs the acts imposed on all imported goods—so smuggling

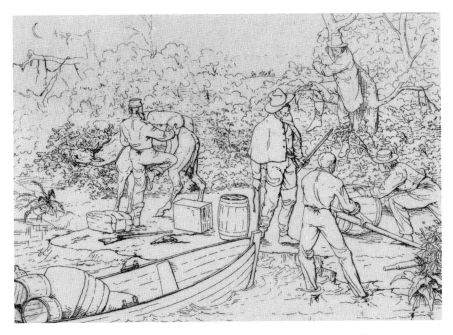

The hundreds of inlets and coves along the Chesapeake meant that smuggling was common. *New York Public Library.*

continued. The colonies' proximity to the islands of the Caribbean (where nearly every European power had at least one trading harbor) made it nearly impossible to keep illegal cargoes from entering the ports.

While Maryland residents certainly made huge profits from illegal cargoes, tiny Rhode Island was the smuggling capital of the colonies. Rhode Island's captains developed a clever way to circumvent British customs officials by exploiting "flags of truce." Such flags were flown when ships from warring nations exchanged prisoners, and canny merchants bought these flags from colonial governors, hired French speakers to pose as prisoners and sailed to the French West Indies to make an exchange of both "prisoners" and valuable cargoes. Pennsylvania governor William Denny sold so many that by 1759 the flags were traded openly on the New York market.[26]

British attempts to control and tax trade backfired—the goods provided to the French West Indies by American smugglers prolonged the British conflict with the French in North America. The increasing tensions between American colonists and their mother country led slowly but inexorably to the Revolutionary War.

In the years leading up to the American Revolution, the warehouses of Fells Point hid shipments of gunpowder and shot; once the conflict burst into the open, Baltimore became a vital transshipment point for the American forces under George Washington.

With its deep-water harbor, adjacent warehouses and proximity to Baltimore, Fells Point was a prime location for illicit activity. Rum, molasses, tea and spices were handed off to small barges that shot off along the dark waterways as soon as they were loaded. The buyers took delivery at a discreet waterfront location, and the untaxed goods vanished into the marketplace.

Both Fells Point and Baltimore held a number of British sympathizers during the war; the waterfront areas of the towns crawled with privateers, pirates, smugglers, shady traders and spies who made the streets of Fells Point into dangerous places once darkness fell.

After the Revolutionary War, smuggling continued—although now it was to avoid local tariffs and taxes. Several families on Smith and Tilghman Islands supplemented their fishing incomes by ferrying cargoes from docks on Maryland's Eastern Shore across to the warehouses of Fells Point, hidden in shipments of fish or oysters. During the years of Prohibition (1919–33), the cargoes were mostly illicit liquor; during World War II, rationed goods were the main inventory, and in the years that followed, everything from guns to drugs to human beings have been smuggled into Fells Point and Baltimore. Once an act of civil disobedience against improperly levied taxes, smuggling has become a vital component of enormous criminal enterprises.

THE WHARF RAT

801 South Ann Street

According to the Historic American Buildings Survey, the property at 801 South Ann Street was originally two tiny row houses built in 1791–94; in the normal course of events, one would have been occupied by the owner and the other by a tenant. The houses were connected at some point in the early nineteenth century, probably around the War of 1812, and the resulting building served a variety of purposes over the years—many of them nefarious.

Its proximity to the warehouses and docks of the harbor made it a prime location for smugglers and pirates to obtain or dispose of goods, and all manner of illicit deals were struck in the rooms that now house the Wharf Rat.

By 1812, the Wharf Rat was probably a tavern of some kind. There is mention of a tavern at or near the location; it was called the "Sign of the Revenue Barge" and had a reputation as a hangout for smugglers and a place for pirates to fence their loot. But even if this refers to another tavern, the Wharf Rat probably drew the same clientele.

According to the various business registers from over the years, the building has housed a number of businesses related to waterfront activities, but tradition holds that most (if not all) of these were fronts for illegal activities. This is certainly borne out by the story of one of the ghosts in the building, an apparition that is seen in the main bar, near the large fireplace.

The gentleman is never described in much detail—aside from his dark or unremarkable clothing, what people notice are his dead, empty eyes. Most people are so terrified at the sight of him that they turn and bolt from the room. According to oral tradition, he is a former owner of the tavern who crossed someone in a shady business deal and paid with his life. This apparition appears in many photographs, most often as a shadowy blur but occasionally with a bit of frightening detail.

Another ghost dates to the early twentieth century. In 1907, the building contained a saloon and residence owned by Polish immigrant John

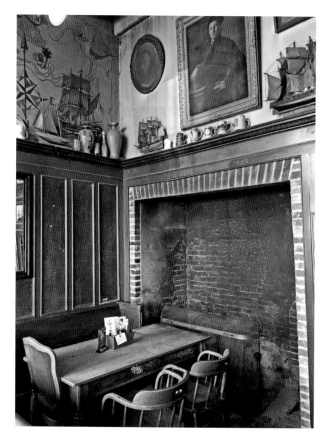

One of the ghosts haunting the Wharf Rat is a man who stands next to this fireplace; when he turns around, his gaze is so terrifying that people flee in horror. *Author photo.*

Rutkowski, whose cousin Joseph owned a similar establishment a few doors down. The population of Fells Point had changed dramatically by this point in history—the narrow houses were filled to bursting with immigrants from eastern Europe, many from Poland. The women worked in the canning factories, and the men supplied cheap labor in the shipyards of Locust Point or sweated in the steel mills.

When there was not enough work, many of the rougher Fells Point denizens turned to drink to pass the time, and on July 19, 1907, John Rutkowski ran afoul of brothers Alexander and Adam Annszewsky. The trial transcript offers no definitive motive for Rutkowski's murder. Some believe the fight was over a woman; in the days leading up to the murder, the girlfriend of one of the Annszewskys was spending an inordinate amount of time at Rutkowski's bar. Another story says that Rutkowski had a Victrola with only one disk—a recording of "The Star-Spangled Banner"—that he played over and over again. Perhaps the Annszewsky brothers were tired of listening to it.

On July 19, 1907, the brothers were in John Rutkowski's saloon in the late morning, drinking and playing pool. According to James Stanton, a principal witness for the prosecution, at two o'clock in the afternoon

> *a fight started in the saloon and ended on the street, when I saw Adam Annszewsky strike John Rutkowski, and both fell to the wall. Hugh Brown struck Alexander Annszewsky and Alexander fell in the gutter. The Annszewskys then went to the saloon of Josph Rutkowski, nearby, and later left. At 4 PM I went to Joseph Rutkowski's saloon and the Annszewskys were in there. I asked Alexander Annszewsky how his jaw was after seeing him spit blood, and he said the man who did it had to die at 5 o'clock. It was then 20 minutes of 5.[27]*

At 5:00 p.m., the Annszewsky brothers—who had purchased a pistol at some point after the initial altercation—returned to John Rutkowski's bar, and Alexander shot him dead.

Whatever led to the fatal argument, it is a fact that watches and clocks in the building sometimes stop dead at 5:00 p.m.; cellphone batteries die, cameras take cloudy pictures and laptop computers shut down without warning—all at 5:00 p.m.

Employees also tell stories of finding dirty tables wiped clean, glasses set out on the counter and the sound of running footsteps behind the bar—perhaps the desperate race to safety that John Rutkowski did not win in 1907.

There are at least two other ghosts in the building, according to staff:

- According to Jen Oliver, an owner of the Wharf Rat, a "woman in white" is often seen, looking out of a second-floor window. The apparition is said to wear a flowing white gown and appears to be middle-aged, instead of in the flower of her youth—many believe her to be the wife of a nineteenth-century businessman, a lady who perhaps also functioned as a madam. Photographs of the second-floor windows often show a woman's face peering out of an otherwise empty room.
- An unidentified spirit likes to play pranks on the staff, tapping them on their shoulders and moving items around. One employee was in an upstairs storage room when he felt a "presence"; catching a glimpse of movement out of the corner of his eye, he looked toward a wall. An array of knives floated in the air, freed

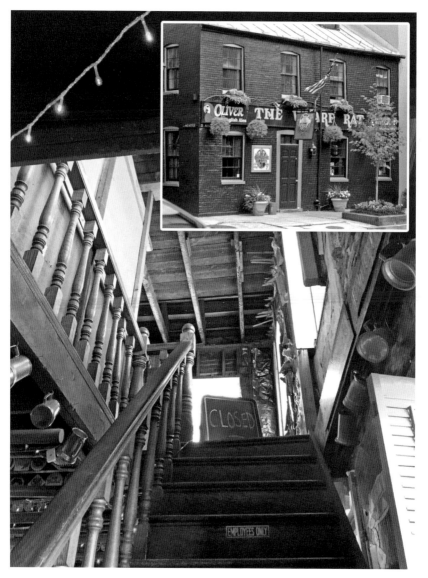

The Wharf Rat's "woman in white" haunts the second floor and has been seen looking out from an upstairs window. *Author photo.*

from the magnetic strip that had held them against the wall. When he gasped in shock, all of the knives fell with a clatter, and he fled the room. On another occasion, the same employee was alone in the bar and the television remote whizzed past his head, just missing him.

7

THE BOOTMAKER'S GHOST

Does it follow that I reject all authority? Perish the thought. In the matter of
boots, I defer to the authority of the boot-maker.
—Mikhail Bakunin (1814–76), Russian political theorist

THE HORSE YOU CAME IN ON

1626 Thames Street

This popular tavern is built on land that was once part of Fells Prospect, the estate of William Fell. His son, Edward, had the land surveyed and divided into lots for sale in 1761–63. Edward Fell's will, which was proved in 1766, described the current site of the tavern as being part of "my mansion house and surrounding property." The original Fell mansion was demolished to accommodate the layout of the new town in the late 1760s; Edward's son William sold the current structure (a three-story building dating to about 1775) to Thomas Usher, a dry goods merchant, in 1782.

A 1791 deed in the chain of title for 1626 Thames describes the property thus:

> [A]*ll that lott of land beginning at a Grave Yard on the south side of Shakespeare*
> *Alley (said Grave Yard being reserved by Edward Fell deceased father of the*
> *said William Fell) and running thence east…the ground including William*

Fells Mansion House…thence bounding on Fells Street South fifty-five degrees West ninety feet to a brick house built by Captain Forbes.

Since its sale in 1775, the building has been listed in the tax rolls as a residence and shop. Thomas Usher's estate sold the building to Edward Hagthrop, a cordwainer (shoemaker); Hagthrop sold it to Erasmus Uhler, a tanner by trade. Uhler's widow sold it to another shoemaker, a man named Matthew Bennet, who operated a shop and grocery on the first floor and had his residence on the floors above from 1822 until 1869.

While there are no documents that list 1626 Thames Street as a tavern prior to the early twentieth century, it was common for businesses to supplement their income by selling liquor by the drink, functioning as de facto saloons. Matthew Bennet, a boot-maker and grocer, definitely sold spirits in the cask or by the bottle, and his shop was an informal drinking place. The previous owners probably did much the same; a lot of liquor—legal and illegal (meaning the excise taxes were not paid)—moved through Fells Point during the nineteenth and twentieth centuries.

The presence of a ghost has been attested to by many current and former employees of the Horse, dating back to the 1960s. The cash register drawer will open, and a large chandelier swings back and forth—sometimes dramatically so—in the absence of any wind or vibration. One bartender had to re-close the cash drawer repeatedly one morning as she prepared for her shift—it popped open whenever she

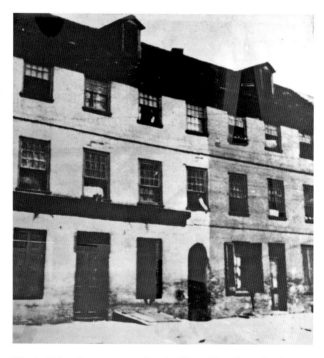

The building that now contains the Horse You Came In On, 1895. *Howard B. Gerber.*

walked past. Recounting her experience to another bartender, she was surprised to hear that he had experienced the same phenomenon on numerous occasions.

Footsteps have been heard echoing across the floors of the rooms above the bar and on a staircase leading to the third floor. In fact, one such story comes from Mike Carter, one of the authors of this book and founder of TOURS & CRAWLS.

As the nephew of the bar's founder and former owner, Mike spent several summers living in a small second-floor bedroom while working as a bar back. The experience that still haunts him (so to speak) came on a night when he was awakened in the late hours by heavy footsteps coming up the stairs.

Mike thought it was his uncle, who'd been enjoying a night out on the town, and called his name in greeting; when the footsteps came down the hallway to stop outside his door, he called out from his bed, "Come in, I have to ask you something!"

There was no reply, so he called again. There was no answer, but he heard the rasping sound of someone turning on their heel, and the heavy steps moved back to the stairwell. He heard the creak of the treads as the unresponsive visitor ascended to the third-floor apartment; there was the familiar creak as the door opened and closed.

Figuring that a night on the town might have rendered his uncle a bit the worse for wear, Mike got out of bed.

> So, I climb out of bed and slide on my shoes—I hated walking barefoot on those old floors—opened my door and went upstairs to find my uncle. I needed a ride back to my parents' house in the morning and wanted to make sure he could take me. Otherwise, I'd have to find another ride. At the time I was only fifteen years old and had no license, let alone a car.
>
> I was surprised to find the door locked. He almost never locked the door, especially when I was there, as I shared his bathroom and kitchen. I had a key, but it was downstairs, so I knocked thinking maybe he had a date with him. He was young and single! There was no answer, not even a "Come back later." I knocked again, this time louder. No answer, but I heard footsteps moving around inside. At this point I was a little freaked out… but also curious. So, I went down and got my key.
>
> While in my room, I could still hear heavy footsteps walking around above me and thought I heard a man's voice, but with so many sounds coming from out on Thames Street, anything was possible. With key in hand I walked back up the stairs, stopped at the door and knocked one last time. Any sound coming from inside instantly stopped. I knew it was

unlikely there was a burglar in the building, as we had an alarm and my uncle had a massive black pet Doberman aptly named Cerberus (as in guardian of the gates of hell), who was also a trained guard dog. Anyway, curiosity got the best of me; I inserted the key into the lock, turned the handle and heard the familiar creak of the old hinges as the door swung open.

No sound was emanating from within. I called for my uncle…no answer. So, I walked inside and looked around. I check all over, every room, the bathroom, kitchen, nothing! There was no one inside. "Weird," I thought to myself. Now, I was very freaked out; I'll admit I was kind of scared, too. I used the bathroom while I was there, grabbed a quick glass of water and then went back down the stairs. Imagine my shock as I turned the corner at the bottom of the upper stairway and ran right into my uncle on the second-floor landing! I literally jumped out of my skin! He jumped a bit himself at my shocked reaction. I told him what had just happened, and he laughed a little and said, "Well, I guess you just met 'Edgar.'" Still a bit shaken, off we went to our respective beds.[28]

A frequent customer reported hearing voices coming from empty areas of the main room on quiet nights, while others tell stories of cold spots, flickering lights and bizarre cellphone behavior such as odd text messages and battery levels that suddenly sink to nothing. Photographs taken inside the bar are sometimes distorted or have unaccounted-for shadows or reflections.

Paranormal investigators have conducted analyses of electromagnetic data and EVP activity gathered from the site; all investigators agreed that the data showed consistent paranormal activity.

According to staff and regular guests, the spirits become personally upset if patrons question their existence; a scoffing comment like "There are no such things as ghosts!" can send your beer bottle off the table or pull a barstool right out from under you. Everyone agrees that the spirits appreciate being acknowledged and greeted; many often call out a greeting to "Edgar." (One of the ghosts in the building is said to be Edgar Allan Poe, who died in Baltimore under mysterious circumstances in 1849).

While Poe's ghost may visit the establishment, he would most likely remain in the bar on the main floor; the ghost that Carter and his uncle encountered upstairs is probably another individual altogether.

Matthew Bennet, boot maker, grocer and informal saloon keeper, lived and worked in the building for over forty years before dying of natural causes in his apartment upstairs; the heavy footsteps could be the old cordwainer returning to his apartment at the end of a day's work—or perhaps a customer is ensuring the quality and fit of a new pair of boots.

Unless they were wealthy, most people could not afford custom-made boots. Premade footwear—known as "sales shoes"—came in only two widths, and there was no difference between right and left. Buying a new pair of boots meant putting them on and stomping around to allow your feet to settle properly, and the shoemaker might even have you step into a bucket of water to soak the leather and allow it to stretch. Some of those heavy footsteps could belong to customers, but surely some of them are the sound of the old bootmaker, Matthew Bennet, keeping an eye on the business and the building that were his for many decades.

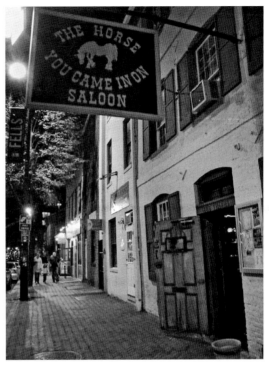

The restaurant and bar is located on land that once contained the home of William Fell, who may also haunt the building. *Author photo.*

There may also be ghosts in the building that go further back in time. The Horse is built on the site of the former Fell family mansion and might be haunted by none other than William Fell, the founder of Fells Point. The home he built in the 1730s was his residence until his death in 1763, and the graveyard holding his remains lies on Shakespeare Street at the rear of the tavern property.

A gentleman in a sober black coat and knee breeches has been seen in the building and at the rear of the property, just outside the fence surrounding the graveyard. Some believe this ghost is the same one that has been spotted walking through the streets of Fells Point, described in another chapter, who is thought to be either Edward or William Fell.

Whatever unquiet spirits haunt the Horse You Came In On Saloon, it doesn't seem to affect the ambiance or the sense of welcome. Whether it's America's spookiest poet, a hardworking boot maker or the founder of Fells Point that's sitting next to you, you never drink alone at the Horse.

8

THE STREETS OF FELLS POINT

It is required of every man…that the spirit within him should walk abroad among his fellow-men, and travel far and wide; and, if that spirit goes not forth in life, it is condemned to do so after death.
—A Christmas Carol, *Charles Dickens (1812–70), English novelist*

When Fells Point was divided into lots by Edward Fell in 1763, he gave names to the streets and alleys of the new town. Ann Street is named for Edward Fell's wife, while another is named for her mother, Aliceanna, whose husband, John Bond, also has a street named for him.

The Fell family originated in Lancashire (Lancaster Street), in the north of England, and Thames, Shakespeare, Exeter and Fleet were names born of nostalgia or in homage to their native country.[29]

The streets of Fells Point were dangerous. A port town attracted and held an unsavory population that preyed on the vulnerable and unprepared—and while most modern Americans are not baffled by large towns or cities, this was not the case during the eighteenth and nineteenth centuries.

At that time, the majority of humanity was born, lived and died within a thirty-mile radius. Merchants and carters might take merchandise into a big city, but farmers and artisans sold their goods at local markets—there was no reason to travel any farther. For many immigrants, the first sight they had of a large town was when they got onto a ship in a major port, and when they disembarked in Boston or New York or Baltimore they were bewildered. Those cities were chaotic melting pots, and few more so than Baltimore.

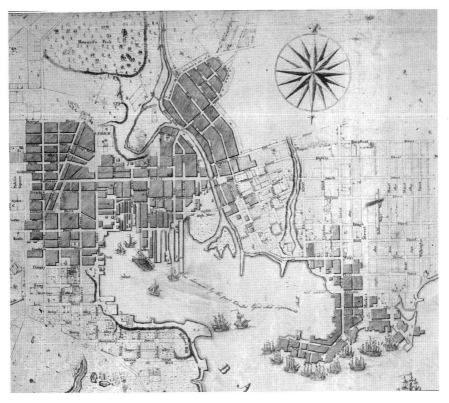

Map of Baltimore and Fells Point, 1792. *New York Public Library.*

English colonists from the Jamestown settlement in Virginia might have arrived in the Patapsco region first, with David Jones opening his mills along the Jones Falls in 1661, but within twenty years the population included Dutch merchants from their settlements along the Delaware River and representatives of trading concerns from all over Europe and the Caribbean. The docks and wharves rang with a thousand different voices: free blacks ran businesses and operated as traders, brightly dressed sailors jostled through the streets, plainly dressed merchants haggled at the shipping factors' offices and food vendors and laden carts argued for space on the crowded roads.

Men of wealth and position had at least one servant to accompany them and possessed letters of introduction that ensured a safe place to stay, but an impoverished or country-bred visitor could only stare like a yokel...prime picking for a variety of harvesters. If they were robbed, "rolled" by a prostitute or otherwise defrauded of their belongings, hapless immigrants were often forced into indentured service to survive. Others were kidnapped and awoke to find themselves on fishing vessels, forced to work hard just to ensure their safe return to land. Still others died within days of arrival—of botched robberies, accidents and disease. Bodies were constantly being recovered from the water near the wharves—some belonging to sailors incapacitated by drink, while others were marked by knife slashes or other injuries. The newspapers from nineteenth-century Baltimore contain many accounts of these victims, some of whom were never identified, who died at the hands of persons unknown.

Women arrived in the colonies as wives, children or indentured servants. Wives and children generally belonged to the moneyed classes and were carefully escorted from the docks by husbands or relatives; working-class women generally traveled with their spouses. Young women who committed themselves to a term of indenture were met at the docks and escorted to the offices of the labor factor that had paid for their ticket; the factor would then sell their indentures and they would serve five to seven years in domestic service, receiving room, board and a very small stipend. When their terms had finished, women were often put out on the streets and replaced by another indentured servant because it was less expensive than paying a living wage.

If a free woman had no real skills, there was little for her to do but become a prostitute or turn to some form of criminal activity or affiliation to survive. Some of the "ladies" of Fells Point were as dangerous as the men. They drugged and robbed their customers, colluded with male accomplices to kidnap drunken sailors, fenced stolen goods and killed informants.

Many female ghosts wander the streets of the Point, especially those that are directly adjacent to Thames Street, the main thoroughfare along the wharves. A number of stories describe figures glimpsed as they move down alleys, stand on street corners or drift among the docks and wharves. Pale young women in long skirts and low, scoop-necked chemises beckon from shadowy alleys, a hard-faced woman wearing a long cloak stalks down Fell Street and a slender girl holding a baby sits on the steps of a house on Bethel. Some of the ghosts appear to come from later in history—a young African American woman in a dress from the early twentieth century walks down Dallas on unsteady feet, singing to herself; a factory girl from World War I disappears into an alley off Exeter; and a very young dark-skinned girl in a tartan skirt and starched shirt skips rope along High Street, her long pigtails bouncing.

Of course, the streets were not much safer for men, and a number of male ghosts have been seen over the years, many of whom appear to have bloody injuries or are dressed in dripping clothing, with their wet hair clinging to

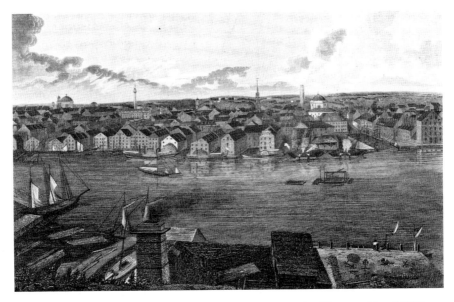

The harbor area was packed with buildings in 1830, but few survive. The great Fire of 1904 destroyed much of Baltimore's port area, but the Fells Point's wharves survived. *Author photo.*

their faces. Most famous are the "five drowned sailors" that walk up Ann and Fell Streets as if coming from the harbor; clothes and hair dripping, their white faces and sunken eyes have terrified a number of people and prompted calls to 911. (See the entry for the Robert Long House in the next chapter for more on this story.)

In many other cases, the apparitions are not frightening—in fact, people generally assume they are seeing a living history reenactor or merely an unconventional Fells Point resident (not uncommon!). Men in sailor costume standing on wharves, leaning on old warehouse buildings and seated on bulkheads and piers are reported frequently, as are Union officers from the Civil War era and American soldiers from World War I.

One ghost does more than just lean on a building or haunt a single street: this gentleman strolls through Fells Point as if enjoying an evening walk in pleasant weather, his black coattails hanging below the hands he clasps behind himself, white stockings gleaming beneath the dark fabric of his breeches, tricornered hat neatly set on his dark hair.

One woman who reported seeing this figure was walking east on Aliceanna late one summer night. "About 2:30 a.m., I saw this man dressed in funny clothes like you would see in an old picture like from the eighteenth century," she said. At the time, she was accompanied by her boyfriend, and she called his attention to the man, who continued to walk toward them for a moment before turning between two houses. When they drew opposite the alley a second later, there was no one to be seen.

Others have seen the same man along Lancaster, South Caroline, Thames and Shakespeare; some say that the figure is wandering aimlessly, others that he is moving purposefully, as if enjoying a brisk walk. Sightings have been reported since the late eighteenth century, and nearly everyone agrees that his last name is Fell. Opinion is divided on whether it is Edward (who died suddenly at thirty-three in 1766) or his son William, whose resemblance to his father was marked and who also died quite young, at the age of thirty-seven. Their reasons for haunting the area would be very different.

After long years of argument and persuasion, Edward Fell got his father's consent to lay out a town and begin selling lots. Just at the moment it began to come together, Edward died (of a heart attack or stroke). Perhaps he walks the streets of the city that he never knew in life.

If the ghost is William, perhaps he is consumed by regret for all that he did not do. Edward's son wasn't very successful; when William died, his

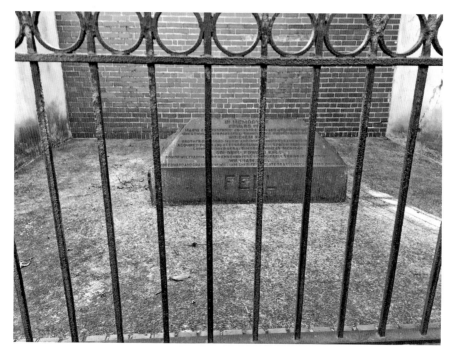

The Fell family graveyard on Shakespeare. A mysterious pedestrian clad in eighteenth-century attire is often seen strolling in the immediate area. *Author photo.*

will was contested by relatives who argued that he was a man in a "weak state of mind." He was seen as dissolute—an unworthy successor to his vigorous father. If William Fell walks the streets near his family's grave site on Shakespeare Street, perhaps he feels guilty that he left no heir. (There are other people named Fell in Maryland and Baltimore history, but this branch came to an end with young William.) Perhaps the streets of Fells Point are haunted by his sense of failure.

713 SOUTH ANN STREET

This restored building, once the home of prominent sea captain Patrick Travis, was built around 1800. The figure of a bearded man wearing a dark coat and blue breeches is frequently spotted in the back lot, which is visible from Durham Street. The man is said to be smoking a pipe and has been known to wave at those who pass him by—only to vanish as the gesture is returned.

516–20 DALLAS STREET

In 1891, a seventy-three-year-old Frederick Douglass visited Baltimore and found that the Bethel AME Church he'd attended as a young man now stood empty. He purchased the building and demolished it, using the site to build five new row houses intended for the poor of Strawberry Alley (now Dallas Street). The houses, which still stand, are two stories and have almost no ornamentation, but 520 Dallas Street has a block of marble set into the wall that bears the name "Douglass Place."

Several ghost sightings have taken place on the street directly in front of these row homes; most often sighted is an elderly African American gentleman, who seems to be leaning on a cane, his gaze fixed on a point at the corner of Dallas and Fleet Streets. No one knows whom (or what) he is waiting for.

9

A HANDFUL OF HAUNTINGS

*The spirit-world around this world of sense
Floats like an atmosphere, and everywhere
Wafts through these earthly mists and vapours dense
A vital breath of more ethereal air.*
—*"Haunted Houses," Henry Wadsworth Longfellow (1807–82), American poet*

ROBERT LONG HOUSE

812 South Ann Street

Located just off Thames Street (and therefore quite convenient to the harbor) this house is the oldest urban residence in Baltimore. It was constructed around 1765 for merchant Robert Long, and the building probably reflects a bit of homesickness on the part of Mr. Long: it resembles the architecture of his birthplace in southeast Pennsylvania.[30] The original interior reflected the wealth and position of its owner; indeed, in 1780, with George Washington's troops in dire need of provisions, Long possessed enough money and clout to commandeer grain (and the carts in which to carry it) and have it shipped to New Jersey.*

---

* Long litigated for years after the Revolution, repeatedly petitioning Congress for repayment of the sums he claimed to have paid out for cart rental and grain. He eventually received some settlement.

In 1774, the merchant married Mary Norwood, and the two lived in the house on Ann Street for a number of years. By 1783, Robert Long had become so successful that he sold the house and several adjoining lots on Ann Street and moved his family to Baltimore County, where he increased his fortune through the purchase of property confiscated from supporters of the English king.[31]

By 1800, the home was owned jointly by Matthew Travers and his brother, Henry, both sea captains commanding ships that crisscrossed the Atlantic, exchanging cargoes of French wine and luxury items for coffee and sugar in the West Indies. Both were independently minded, entrepreneurial in spirit and often flexible in how they interpreted the orders of their ships' owners. Henry Travers was sued by an employer for not following the instructions he had been given, while Matthew Travers once encountered a ship abandoned at sea and, after some dangerous maneuvers, managed to tow it into Savannah, where he sold it for a considerable profit and shared none of the proceeds with his ship's owner.

Both of the Travers brothers captained ships for James Biays, a prominent Fells Point shipbuilder, and Matthew married James's younger sister, Jane. The two were living at 812 South Ann by 1803, and over the next eight years, the couple had four daughters and appear to have been relatively prosperous. But the life of a sea captain is dangerous—Matthew disappeared on a voyage in 1811, lost with both ship and cargo.

Fortunately for Jane, her brother Joseph Biays had taken steps to protect her in just such an eventuality: prior to Matthew's disappearance, Joseph insisted on the creation of a trust that would secure the house against creditors in the case of Matthew's death. Matthew did leave some debts, but Jane kept her home.

Jane appears very seldom in the public record, save in the tax records and in a 1797 petition to the mayor and city council concerning the pools of fetid water that accumulated on George Street. Her brother James, a prominent and wealthy merchant, signed the petition as well.[32] By the few accounts available, she educated her daughters at home and was known as a thoughtful neighbor who bore her widowhood with grace.

As a member of the Biays family, Jane enjoyed a certain prominence, but she does not seem to have had much money of her own. During her residency, Jane was forced to sell pieces of her property to raise money; at her death in 1845, the lot measured only the width of the house (and she was forced to share one chimney with a neighbor).

In the century that followed Jane's death, the house went through a number of owners but was used principally as a residence. (During the late nineteenth

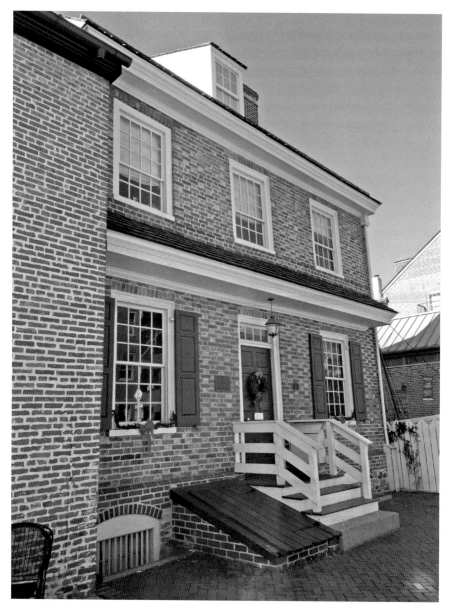

The oldest urban residence in Baltimore, the Robert Long House has been carefully restored to its former glory. *Author photo.*

century, the third floor attic was expanded, and the building was subdivided into apartments.) Like the neighborhood around it, the house slowly decayed, and in 1973, it was purchased for only $9,000 by the Fells Point Historical Society.

Initially unaware of its history, the society had purchased the building because it was in sound enough condition to be thoroughly restored, incorrectly estimating the date of construction to be some time after the American Revolution. A meticulous investigation into the building's origins revealed its beginnings, and once volunteers managed to peel off the tar-based sealant that coated the exterior, the hand-made bricks, glazed headers and meticulous mortar could be seen. The third floor, which had been grafted onto the building in the late nineteenth century, was removed to reveal the original two-story house, with its pent roof over the attic and four brick chimneys. The society restored the building, opening the ground floor to public tours and using the upper floors as administrative space and offices.

In the years since the house was opened to the public, many staff and visitors have reported odd events and strange encounters. One of the most active areas seems to be the stairs leading to the second floor; whether ascending or descending, visitors feel a gentle brush of icy fingers on a shoulder or a momentary clasp on an arm, while others encounter intense cold spots or hear a woman's voice. There have been frequent sightings of a woman in a long skirt moving up the staircase or through the rooms on the main floor; many visitors assume the figure is a living history actor and have been known to ask staff if she would be willing to come back and pose for a photograph. So far, she has not honored these requests.

A second-floor bedroom at the back of the home has been the site of many episodes, with reports of moving objects, flickering lights and the sound of a woman's voice, along with intense cold spots that are located on or near the bed. Residents of buildings that stand at the back of the lot have seen a woman's face looking out of the bedroom window, and people standing in the courtyard behind the house have reported similar phenomena.

Paranormal investigators have reported strong readings inside the house, particularly in the back bedroom, where EMF readings center most strongly about the area of the bed. Various mediums have claimed that a ghost named "Mary" is haunting the house, and some speculate that she is none other than Mary Norwood Long. This seems unlikely, because Robert Long's wife had not lived in the house for at least two years prior to her death, which took place at Long's Baltimore country estate.

The likeliest candidate is Jane Biays Travers, who lived at 812 South Ann longer than anyone else and whose ties to the property run the deepest. Her continuing presence in the building might explain another haunting associated with it: the five drowned sailors.

On a dark winter evening in the 1990s, the director of the Fells Point Historical Society was working in her attic office when she heard the sound of the heavy door knocker thud against the door to South Ann Street. She went to the window and looked down but saw no one standing on the stoop, which was directly below her. Concluding that she'd heard an echo from the street or perhaps that a child was playing jokes, she went back to work; a few moments later, the knocking was repeated. She decided to go down to answer the door, and as she descended the staircase, the knocker sounded again.

When she opened the door, she saw what she described as "full apparitions of five sailors who had obviously drowned." That they were aware of her presence was obvious...water dripped from their hair and uniforms as they beckoned to her from the sidewalk, gesturing for her to join them. Her heart pounding in terror, she slammed the door shut and locked it before retreating to her office and making a few phone calls. Other staff and volunteers have heard the door knocker sound at night, but in light of her experience, none of them was willing to open the door!

The same quintet, whose blue-and-white shirts recall those worn by eighteenth- and nineteenth-century sailors, has been reported at locations along Thames Street, which fronts the once-teeming wharves of the old harbor. Their appearance inspires both terror and disbelief, and several modern bars along Thames have had customers who come in for a restorative beverage after an encounter; nearly all of them call a taxi when it is time to go home because they don't want to risk another meeting.

While the sailors' identities are unknown, it is impossible not to speculate that they are perhaps connected with the disappearance of Jane's husband, Captain Matthew Travers. Perhaps they bring a message from her vanished partner, or perhaps they hold him responsible for their deaths...and have come to demand a reckoning.

MAX'S TAPHOUSE

737 South Broadway

Constructed between 1870 and 1910, the building that houses Max's Taphouse of Broadway and Lancaster Streets contains a number of ghosts. The owner, Ron Furman, is a bit skeptical of the paranormal, but even he was spooked when a member of his staff came out of the basement in hysterics, babbling about decapitated chickens running amok. The members of the kitchen staff remained wary of the basement, but Furman didn't think there was much to it—after all, nobody else had seen headless chickens. But twenty-three years later, he discovered that his building had once been used as a grocery or butcher shop, and chickens had been routinely slaughtered in his basement.

Like many buildings throughout historic districts, the foundations of Max's Taphouse are the oldest part of it because new construction often incorporated preexisting foundations. There is no record of what previously occupied the site, but given its location on Broadway it was most likely a large shop or sales office with living quarters upstairs. It is also possible that the location was occupied by a tavern and rooming house during the early years of Fells Point.

Paranormal events seem to connect to locations, not objects (there are obvious exceptions); when a building is demolished and replaced with another, the ghost doesn't climb into the dump truck with the construction debris and relocate. If that means that a former hallway is now bisected by a wall, the ghost walks through the wall; if a stairway is now placed on the opposite side of a room, the ghost ignores it and uses an invisible staircase to climb to the next floor. During renovations of this property, several interior walls were removed on the ground floor and others created; many of the ghost sightings involve an apparition that walks into or out of a solid wall.

Patrons and employees at Max's have reported seeing a man walk through one of the walls of the main bar. He appears to be dressed in a dark suit whose description would match the dark and plain professional attire of a storekeeper or merchant in the eighteenth century. (Many early merchants in Fells Point were Quakers.)

There have also been reports of a "woman in white" who drifts through the bar. She doesn't fade through a wall…she just vanishes. As the property was used as a grocery during the late nineteenth and early twentieth centuries, it is possible that she is a shop girl or a member of the owner's family, who would have lived upstairs. It is also possible that she may come from an earlier point in the building's history.

Duda's

1600 Thames Street

The building at the corner of Thames and Bond Streets is one of the few triangular buildings in Fells Point and was most likely constructed in the early nineteenth century. According to local lore, the building was a hotel for sailors; the rounded exterior angles of the building deflected evil spirits, by some maritime superstitions. By the 1880s, it was occupied by the Maryland Bay Pilots Association. At some point in the early twentieth century, the address is said to be occupied by a rooming house for sailors, but following the end of Prohibition, it became a bar. Walter Duda took over the location in 1949, and it is still being operated by his descendants.

The bar is said to be haunted by the ghost of a retired merchant seaman who lived (and died) in an upstairs apartment in the building. "Doc" was a mainstay at the bar, and he was a really nice guy…but he had a habit that drove people crazy.

Doc had a favorite polka song on the jukebox, and he played it over and over again. After his death in the 1980s, the 45 rpm record was ceremonially removed from the jukebox, but to the shock of the customers and staff, every now and then that familiar tune would start playing…a reminder that Doc was still keeping an eye on the place.

Patrons and employees still hear the sounds of that polka echoing through the bar, even though the jukebox has been gone for a very long time. Other activities have also been reported, both upstairs and down: objects moving, the sound of footsteps and doors that open and close. Are these lodgers from long ago or more modern customers that just can't leave their favorite bar behind?

1904–6 Aliceanna Street

There are many stories that have appeared historically in newspapers and magazines concerning local ghosts and haunted houses; sadly, many of the buildings referenced in those stories were destroyed in the re-development in Fells Point in the twentieth century. But it seems likely that one of these still-existing adjoining row homes is the subject of the following story, from the *Baltimore Sun* of September 11, 1919.

Despite the shortage of houses, there's a house in this city in which no one will live. There's only one thing the matter with the house—it is said to be haunted.

The house is on Aliceanna Street, between Wolfe and Washington. Of course, the neighborhood isn't what it used to be; neither is the house. A few windows are broken, the door is boarded up and the red paint is rather rusty-looking, but that's probably because no one has lived in the place for two years. It is safe to say, though, that a tenant with the temerity to brave the "ghosts" will not be bothered with high rent, and probably will not have to worry about moving out to allow a better-paying tenant to move in.

Back in the days when Aliceanna Street was the leading residential street of that part of the city the house was occupied.

Now the only sound is the eerie tramp of the ghost. Whose ghost it is no one seems to know, but that there is a ghost is common gossip in the neighborhood. The unearthly visitor is said to make periodical pilgrimages to the scene. A light has been seen shining through the windows about midnight, which is the time all ghosts prowl.

At least a half-dozen families are sure about the ghost. They have every reason to know because, at various times, during the past two years, they have moved into the house. But they never stayed long. One or two visits from the ghost was enough and they moved out.

Some say the ghost is that of a miser who lived there in seclusion. Others say the ghost is that of a witch and that she visits the house by coming down the chimney. Both may be right but all who have attempted to live in the house are sure about the ghost.

These row homes, constructed in the 1790s, have been occupied by a variety of residents over the centuries; records indicate that 1906 Aliceanna has had a high turnover in both owners and tenants, but whether or not a ghost drove them out is open to question.

10

POE IN BALTIMORE

The boundaries which divide life from death are at best shadowy and vague. Who shall say where the one ends, and where the other begins?
—*Edgar Allan Poe, "The Premature Burial"*

Somehow, somewhere, the story got started that Edgar Allan Poe liked to drink at a tavern at 1626 Thames Street. Now the site of the Horse You Came In On Saloon, this property is often identified as the place where the poet imbibed his final drink before stumbling into a gutter in a fatal alcoholic stupor. It's sad to cast doubt on such an excellent story, but a man named Matthew Bennet was operating a boot shop at that address in 1849, and Poe was found in a tavern on Lombard Street, nearly half a mile away.

It's natural that a Fells Point bar wants to claim Edgar as its resident ghost—Poe was no stranger to the bars of Fells Point. In the early 1830s, he lived on what was called Mechanic's Row, in a house that no longer exists; a few years later, he was living across town at 203 North Amity Street, where he wrote some of his early works. But by 1849, he hadn't been a resident for years—and he wasn't supposed to be in Baltimore in the first place: Poe was on his way to Philadelphia! No one really knows what led to his death; it's a mystery that has fascinated the public and scholars since 1849.

Did Poe, who had given up drinking, return to alcohol? Was he on drugs? Did he die of some fever in his brain? There are a number of theories, but here are some facts (and a little bit of speculation). What follows is taken from a timeline put together by the Edgar Allan Poe Society of Baltimore.

On June 29, 1849, Edgar Allan Poe left New York on a lecture tour to raise money and interest in a new magazine he was attempting to launch that was to be called *Stylus*. On a stop in Richmond, Virginia, he renewed his acquaintance with Elmira Shelton, a childhood sweetheart now widowed like him. (Poe's wife, Virginia, had died in 1847.)

Evidently, love bloomed anew. There was talk of an engagement; he discussed moving to Richmond and was sober and in good spirits. On September 27, 1849, he had a late supper in Richmond with friends who walked him to the docks, where he got onto a ship destined for Baltimore. But once he arrived, he did not take the train to Philadelphia, where he had an appointment. He vanished that very evening, after calling on a few Baltimore friends.

No one knew where he was until the evening of October 3, 1849, when a Baltimore voter named Joseph W. Walker sent this note to Dr. J.E. Snodgrass, a friend of Poe's:

> *Dear Sir, There is a gentleman, rather the worse for wear, at Ryan's 4th ward polls, who goes under the cognomen of Edgar A. Poe, and who appears in great distress, & he says he is acquainted with you, and I assure you, he is in need of immediate assistance, Yours, in haste, Jos. W. Walker.*

Located in a tavern known as "Gunner's Hall," Ryan's 4th Ward Polls was the name of an election site. (Taverns were commonly used as polling places, leading to a lot of free drinks if you voted for the right candidate.) Gunner's Hall was located on South Lombard Street between High and Exeter; the building was demolished long ago, and modern housing now occupies the block. This tavern was quite a distance from 1626 Thames Street, and by Dr. Snodgrass's account, Poe was in no condition to walk.

Dr. Snodgrass was convinced that Poe had gone on a drinking binge (he had struggled with alcohol for years), but there were signs that something more might have happened. He was dressed in cheap, filthy clothing and wearing the flimsiest of shoes; he had no money and none of his personal effects (except, oddly, the Malacca sword cane of a Richmond acquaintance that Poe apparently had grabbed by mistake before taking the boat). Poe lapsed in and out of consciousness, complaining of head pain, before dying at Washington College Hospital in the early hours of the morning on October 7, 1849.

The mystery of why he was in Baltimore is compounded by questions about where he had been and what caused his death. Alcoholism, malaria, poisoning and even rabies have been proposed by various authorities. One of the more recent theories is compelling and may answer the question of why Poe was found in a polling place, dressed in the clothes of a vagrant, incoherent and covered in bruises.

Baltimore was in the throes of an election, and the streets were filled with adherents of one candidate or another; fueled by alcohol, the scene was raucous, and it was common to see men engaging in fisticuffs (what you might call spirited political argument) outside the polling places. Ward politics could be dirty, and one of the unsavory ways elections were rigged was by "cooping," a practice that involved abducting vulnerable men of voting age and forcing them to vote repeatedly in multiple precincts. The abductees (who were usually strangers with no local connections) were often controlled by the administration of opiates or alcohol and the use of physical violence; incoherent and incapable of true resistance, they were stripped and re-costumed in a variety of clothing to further the deception. These men were kept in "coops," probably referring to a cheap room in a stable or warehouse, and taken from precinct to precinct until the polls closed.

Poe got off his ship in Baltimore and made a few social calls before vanishing on the evening of his arrival. Is it possible that he was snatched off the streets of Fells Point, held in a coop, drugged with opiates or alcohol and forced to vote? Or did he go on an epic bender and wind up vagrant and penniless after a mugging? There's no way to know for sure.

While no one saw Edgar Allan Poe anywhere near 1626 Thames Street on the night he was found at Gunner's Hall, many residents (and employees of the Horse You Came In On) are convinced that one of America's most famous poets wanders the streets of Fells Point and stops in for an occasional beverage…and there's certainly no reason he shouldn't join the rest of the ghosts that still call Fells Point home.

11

PIRATES AND PRIVATEERS

If England had not used the services of privateers and pirates during its long struggle with Spain, there is some likelihood that people today in North America would be speaking Spanish rather than English.
—*Robert Earl Lee*, Blackbeard the Pirate: A Reappraisal of His Life and Times

With its maritime history, Fells Point boasts any number of privateers and pirates as former residents—and undoubtedly, some of the seafaring ghosts that people see took their turns on ships that searched the sea for conflict and plunder. But pirates were lawbreakers, and privateers were patriots—or at least that's what history tells us.

THE LIFE OF A BALTIMORE PRIVATEER

The eighteenth- and nineteenth-century harbors of Baltimore and Fells Point teemed with colorful characters, but few were as lauded and famous as the privateers who attacked British shipping and Royal Navy vessels during the American Revolution and War of 1812. Sailing under letters of authority from the government, these dashing captains and their well-trained crews preyed on enemy shipping, ran harbor blockades and engaged enemy warships—often using their intimate knowledge of local shoals and tides to force the vessels toward the shore, where they were boarded or destroyed. The profits from such captures were shared among the owners, captain, crew and the government that issued the ship's papers, and the profits could be enormous—small wonder that so many sailors were eager to sign on for a privateering voyage.

A "letter of marque" was granted to a merchant vessel, to be used if the opportunity arose, but a commissioned privateer ship carried no cargo, was armed to the teeth and skillfully crewed by highly experienced seamen.[33] In both cases, the primary target was merchant shipping that flew the flag of the nation against whom the commission had been issued.

The ships and cargoes that were seized were sold and the profit—which was known as "prize money"—split between the government and the ship's owners, captain and crew. Passengers and crew aboard a seized vessel were generally immediately released, but crew aboard military vessels were often taken back to port and held for ransom or exchange.

Most of the seafaring nations of Europe issued these commissions, but they didn't do so because they needed ships to attack another nation's navy—no trading ship would willingly go up against a heavily armed frigate, and privateers didn't want to take on such a dangerous target either. Such commissions were granted solely to deprive an enemy of resources by restricting trade, tie up military vessels and cripple the economy.[34]

Both privateering commissions and letters of marque were used by American captains during the American Revolution, inflicting damage to British shipping that grew exponentially as increasing numbers of American ships prowled the waters. Many privateers returned empty-handed from a voyage, but a small number of successful captains brought in prize after prize, often growing fabulously wealthy.[35]

A successful captain needed more than skill at navigation and knowledge of the shipping lanes—he required a ship built for speed and the services of a veteran crew. The shipyards of Fells Point provided the vessels and a ready supply of experienced seamen eager for prize money. By the end of the American Revolution, Fells Point was a major shipbuilding center, with a number of skilled shipwrights; in 1794, some 34 percent of the inhabitants were involved in building, fitting and sailing ships. But the true fame of the shipyards rested on the astonishing speed of a ship whose design and attributes are recognized around the world.

The ship that was known as a "Baltimore Flyer" had two sharply raked (tilted) masts that allowed sails to be set to precise angles—focusing every breath of wind as the captain directed—and a narrow hull that sliced through water.* At a time when the average merchant vessel or fully armed military frigate averaged five to seven knots at sea, the ship nicknamed the "Yankee Racehorse" could make nearly twice as much, and an experienced captain could change course in a fraction of the time a larger, more cumbersome ship required.

The sight of that distinctively angled silhouette under full sail was cursed by every pirate, privateer and military vessel that watched it vanish swiftly over the horizon, nearly uncatchable. Sailing these ships required a special touch at the helm; if one was captured, the ship often capsized or was blown onto shoal or shore because captain and crew did not know how to handle it. While they did not handle large cargoes, speed and maneuverability made the Yankee Racehorse the ship of choice for many American privateers who saw conflict with Great Britain as an opportunity to make a fortune during the War of 1812.

The United States might not have become involved in the final agonies of the Napoleonic Wars if Congress had delayed its vote for a week or two. The main argument for going to war—British Orders in Council that hamstrung American trade and allowed for the seizure of American sailors—had been repealed, but word arrived too late. The United States was in no mood to back down, and besides, U.S. general William Huff had already begun an invasion of British Canada.[36] Quite a number of Americans were interested in acquiring the territories to the north and saw an opportunity to drive the British out of North America.[37]

Throughout the conflict, the shipyards of Fells Point turned out a number of ships operating under privateering commissions from the U.S. government.** In a two-year span, fifty-six privateers built in Fells Point captured or destroyed over five hundred British vessels. Perhaps the most famous, the privateer *Chasseur*, built in the Point by Thomas Kemp, was responsible for the capture or destruction of many British vessels in the War of 1812. Thomas Boyle, captain of the *Chasseur* in 1814–15, terrorized shipping along the coast of England for three months, going so far as to issue a proclamation that declared an American blockade of Great Britain.[38] After capturing eighteen prizes along the coasts of Ireland and western England, Boyle returned to Fells Point in triumph, and the *Chasseur* was hailed as the "Pride of Baltimore."[39]

---

* The "Baltimore Clipper" came into being well after the war and was a much larger ship designed to carry bulk cargoes, but like its predecessor, it was built for speed and utilized raked masts.
** One of the first commissions issued in the War of 1812 was to a group of Baltimore businessmen, who armed a schooner with ten twelve-pound carronades and persuaded Revolutionary War hero Joshua Barney to sign on as captain. In ninety-eight days at sea in 1812, Barney captured eighteen British merchant ships with a total value of $1.5 million, or $40 million in 2012 dollars.

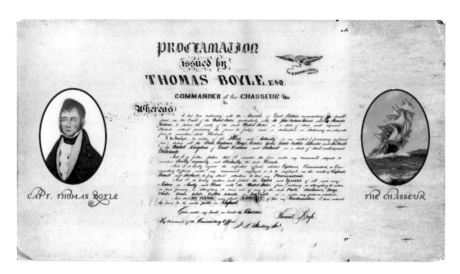

Baltimore privateer Thomas Boyle captured or sank eighteen British ships off the coast of Great Britain, and his proclamation of a blockade of the British Isles infuriated the British, who determined that they must destroy the shipyards at Fells Point.

Boyle's proclamation, which he had given to a captured British captain for publication, was posted on the wall of Lloyd's Coffee House, where it created an immediate sense of panic among British merchants. Shipping costs skyrocketed, insurance rates soared and the Royal Navy was forced to divert fourteen sloops of war and three frigates to patrol the northern and western coasts of England.

British naval forces were already conducting a blockade of American harbors; in response to public outrage—and to demonstrate the overwhelming power of their navy—the British decided combine a strike at the Fells Point privateers with an attack on the heart of American government.

In mid-August 1814, the British attacked and burned Washington, D.C., and then sailed toward Baltimore, intending to burn the shipyards of Fells Point. But word of their intentions sped before the fleet; the citizens of Baltimore had almost three weeks to prepare, and the city became a hive of feverish activity.

Fort McHenry was stocked with ammunition and provisions, and the star-shaped perimeter was raised and buffered against shells. Four smaller fortifications were erected along the waterfront, and a three-mile-long earthwork was raised to guard the city to the northeast. More than fifteen thousand soldiers, militia and irregulars manned the fortifications; observation posts and small ships reported on the advance of the British fleet.

The battle for Baltimore began on September 12, 1814, with British forces landing at North Point while warships conducted a bombardment of Fort McHenry and the harbor defenses. Once the American forces were overcome, the British planned to send marines ashore to burn the shipyards, but the harbor fortifications were too strong and the land attack ended in retreat. The British decided on an all-out artillery assault from their massed warships, training their guns on Fort McHenry. The bombardment lasted through the night, but when dawn arrived, the failure of the British assault was obvious, and the fleet sailed south, where it was defeated in the Battle of New Orleans.[40]

However valiant its defense had been, the end of the war meant an end to Baltimore's prominence as a port, and falling prices for commodities contributed to the collapse of many Baltimore merchant houses. There was a surplus of vessels, and as shipping costs fell dramatically, larger cargo vessels out of New York, Boston and Wilmington secured most of the contracts; the smaller "Baltimore Flyers" were no longer profitable unless they were used in the slave trade or handled perishable cargo that required a swift voyage.

But there was another way to make such a ship profitable, if the owners could be persuaded to place the vessel under the flag of another country. In 1816, while the European continent took a deep breath and began to rebuild from almost twenty years of war, the people of Central and South America decided it was time to press the case for their own independence. None of these nations possessed a navy, and recruiters visited Baltimore to seek out captains willing to enter the service of the revolutions.[41]

A number of Baltimore ships went south; some were sold outright to the revolutionaries, but several captains who maintained residence in Fells Point became embroiled in the struggle, commanding vessels in actions against ships and cities in South America. Venezuela, Mexico and Colombia were in rebellion against Spain, and the Banda Oriental (modern Uruguay) was in revolt against Spain and Portugal. (A ship sailing under a commission from rebel general José Artigas could thus act against vessels of both nations.) These wars created chaos in the Caribbean, as Spanish and Portuguese vessels attacked—and were attacked by—the privateer navies of the colonial rebels that were feasting on merchant shipping.

Captured cargoes were taken to the colonies of small European powers; Dutch-, Swedish- and Danish-held islands profited mightily from the sale of both cargoes and vessels, a situation that continued until 1826, when the governments in Colombia and Venezuela ceased to issue privateering commissions and Portuguese-supported forces defeated the revolutionaries in the Banda Oriental.

In 1856, most European nations signed the Paris Declaration, which abolished privateer commissions and letters of marque; the United States and Spain, along with many South American countries, did not sign, although during the American Civil War and the Spanish-American War, U.S. officials declared their intent to abide by the terms of the declaration.[42]

The age of the privateer was at an end.

THE LIFE OF A PIRATE

It's better to swim in the sea below
Than to swing in the air and feed the crow,
Says jolly Ned Teach of Bristol.
—Benjamin Franklin

In an honest service there is thin commons, low wages, and hard labor;
in this, plenty and satiety, pleasure and ease, liberty and power; and who
would not balance creditor on this side, when all the hazard that is run for
it, at worst, is only a sour look or two at choking. No, a merry life and a
short one, shall be my motto.
—Bartholomew "Black Bart" Roberts

At some point, nearly everybody thinks pirates are cool. Thanks to Hollywood and popular fiction, the image of a swashbuckling mercenary with a heart of gold and a sympathetic backstory has obscured any true portraits of the men and women who plundered on the high seas, very few of whom resembled movie stars. The life of a real pirate was usually brief; death could come from an accident at sea, the struggle to capture a ship, a hangman's noose or the hands of his captain or shipmates.

Piracy can be loosely defined as "an act of robbery on the seas," and the struggle against piracy has existed since the moment trade began.[43] In the modern day, the term is applied to an act of robbery committed on an independently functioning transportation vehicle (ships, submarines

THE PROVINCE OF MARYLAND HEREBY CONDEMNS

THE ACTS OF

EGREGIOUS MURDER AND PIRACY

BY THE

Captain, Mate, AND Crew

OF THE

COCKATRICE OF KENT ISLAND
On April 23, 1635

The crew of the Cockatrice, under the command of
Lieutenant Warren, attempted to seize two of Lord
Baltimore's vessels, the St. Helen and the
St. Margaret, on the Pocomoke River, which resulted
in the murder of his Lord's servant, William Ashmore.

LET IT BE KNOWN THAT

Any further attempts by the pirates of Kent Island on
Maryland property will be met with the swiftest and
severest of punishments. For those who tend toward
thievery and bloodshed with no regard for their
fellow man will find no refuge when brought before
the Law of the Land.

Kent Island, under the leadership of William Claiborne, refused to accept
inclusion in the Maryland colony and engaged in armed resistance; colonial
authorities labeled them pirates. Maryland Gazette *Archives.*

and planes) that is carrying passengers, cargo and crew members. United States courts still grapple with the technical questions that accompany a charge of piracy.[*]

Before the advent of gunpowder, seizing a ship often required a small flotilla, but once there were cannons that could inflict damage from afar, often a single well-armed pirate ship could make a capture. Once subdued, a ship would be looted; if he had skilled navigators and crew to spare, the pirate might seize the ship itself, to keep or to sell. Crew and passengers were generally set free or—in some cases—kept for ransom. (Crew members were often invited or forced to join the pirates.) During what is considered the "Golden Age of Piracy" (1650–1730), many pirates had unofficial ties to government officers, who pointed them against their nation's enemies; Anglo-French seamen attacked Spanish shipping and colonies from 1650 to 1680 and found safe harbor among the British-controlled islands.

Once the British East India Company began to make regular voyages, pirates began to prey on the laden cargo ships that sailed along the coast of Africa and to rob Muslim targets in the Indian Ocean and Red Sea. The route they followed became known as the "Pirate Round," and one of the richest pirate hauls in history was made by Captain Henry Every in 1695 when he attacked a fleet of Indian ships carrying Muslim pilgrims to Mecca. The pirates treated their captives with great brutality, indulging in an orgy of rape and torture, which led many of the women to commit suicide to escape the shame. Several of the victims were related to Indian rulers, and the assault outraged Indian authorities, who immediately imprisoned every British citizen and demanded justice. The first international manhunt was launched by the British government and funded by the British East India Company in search of Henry Every, who returned to England and vanished with all his gold; estimates of the value of the cargo range from $250 million to $400 million in 2012 dollars.

Piracy's cost to consumers was high—merchants lost cargoes, nations lost revenue and trade was significantly impacted. The naval fleets of European nations did their best to protect vessels that flew their flags, but as pirates didn't attack armed warships, the best way to capture a pirate ship was when it was at anchor.

---

[*] In 2010, the United States filed piracy charges against five individuals accused of an act of piracy against a U.S. Navy vessel off the Horn of Africa. In this case, *United States v. Said*, the piracy charges were dropped when the defendants argued that they did not commit any robbery. (Their attack was driven off, and they were subsequently captured.)

Most of the piracy that took place in the Chesapeake Bay occurred in its southern waters, where ships loaded with goods could be attacked as they sailed out of the ports of Virginia or southern Maryland. Edward Teach, who is more commonly known as "Blackbeard," used the secluded inlets of the Tidewater to prepare his ships for action; in 1717, he captured a sloop off Cape Charles, Virginia, and there are records that place him in Delaware Bay and on the Potomac River. Other pirates, such as "Calico" Jack Rackham, his lover Anne Bonny, the cross-dressing Mary Read and Stede Bonnet, also raided shipping in the bay, but most preferred to stay out to sea, where they preyed on the large merchant vessels making their way to Europe or the Caribbean.

One of the pirates often mentioned in connection with the Chesapeake Bay is Captain William Kidd, who is rumored to have hidden some of his treasure along its shores. In 1698, sailing as a privateer for the British Crown, he rounded the Cape of Good Hope at the southern tip of Africa and began to search for French vessels, privateers or pirates. With an unhappy crew (many of whom ultimately abandoned him) and no plunder to pay them, Kidd became desperate, attacking arbitrary vessels and torturing crew members; for all his searching, he made only one significant capture: the *Quedagh Merchant*, a vessel packed with silks, spices, gold and other valuable goods.

After sharing out the loot, Kidd and his under-manned vessel set sail to return to North America, but upon arriving in port in the Caribbean, Kidd learned he had been charged with piracy. Convinced that powerful friends would help him prove his innocence, he took passage on a sloop that was sailing to New York.[44]

The loot from the *Quedagh Merchant* is the foundation for the legend of Captain Kidd's treasure. Before surrendering himself to the royal governor of Massachusetts, Kidd entrusted chests of gold and silver to a friend, who buried them on Gardiners Island at the eastern end of Long Island, New York. These were discovered, confiscated and used against him at trial.

Kidd was brought to trial in England for murder and piracy, and despite his belief in his innocence—and without any assistance from those powerful friends—he was found guilty. Many of his contemporaries, as well as a number of modern scholars, believe that he did not receive a fair trial, and it is certainly a fact that one of the key pieces of exculpatory evidence emerged under mysterious circumstances years after the trial. He was hanged on May 23, 1701, at "Execution Dock" in London. During the execution, the hangman's rope broke, and Kidd was hanged on the second

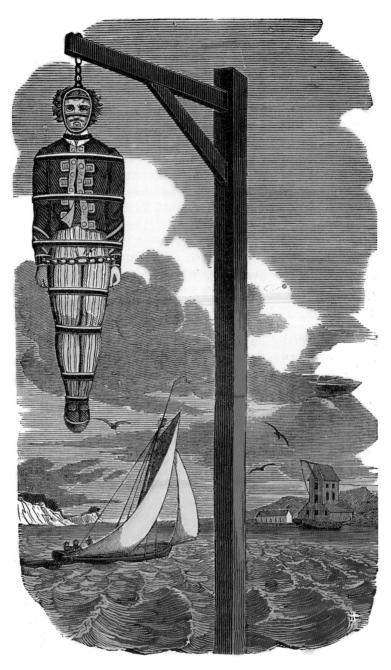

A common method of execution for pirates was to be "hung in irons," exposed to the elements and left to die. Their bodies were left hanging as a warning. *New York Public Library.*

attempt. His body was gibbeted over the River Thames—as a warning to would-be pirates—for three years.

But once the value of the *Quedagh Merchant* and its cargo had been calculated, a significant amount of Kidd's share of the treasure was unaccounted for, and it has long been rumored that he buried a portion somewhere. Treasure hunters seek it to this day.[45] Local legend holds that one of Captain Kidd's booty holds was on a small island in the Chesapeake Bay, now called Gibson Island. Perhaps buried under someone's lawn or under the dark layers of silt lies a small fortune waiting to be found. Or perhaps it already has been discovered. Gibson Island is one of the wealthiest zip codes in all of America.

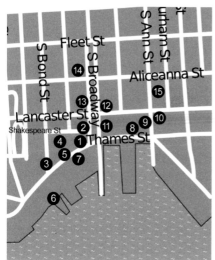

HISTORY & HAUNTINGS IN HISTORIC FELLS POINT

1. ADMIRAL FELL INN: 888 S BROADWAY
2. PROHIBITION ERA SIGN: SHAKESPEARE ST
3. DUDA'S TAVERN: 1600 THAMES ST
4. FELL FAMILY GRAVE: SHAKESPEARE ST
5. THE HORSE YOU CAME IN ON: 1626 THAMES ST
6. FELLS POINT SHIPYARD, RAILWAY & WHARF
7. LEADBETTERS TAVERN: 1639 THAMES ST
8. CAT'S EYE PUB STOP: 1730 THAMES ST
9. ROBERT LONG HOUSE: 812 S ANN ST
10. THE WHARF RAT: 801 S ANN ST
11. RYE BAR: 807 S BROADWAY
12. MAX'S TAPHOUSE: 737 S BROADWAY
13. BERTHA'S MUSSELS: 734 S BROADWAY
14. STICKY RICE (FRIENDS BAR): 1634 ALICEANNA
15. SEA CAPTAIN'S HOUSE: 713 SOUTH ANN ST

Haunted Fells Point. Some buildings are not open to the public; please be respectful of residents as you explore! *Author map.*

Fells Point is constantly changing, and that means that businesses come and go—we can't guarantee that all of the businesses listed are still there. But ghosts don't move out when a new owner moves in, so even if the name has changed, the haunting continues!

Appendix

EXPLORING HAUNTED FELLS POINT

Where given, the numbers here correspond to the map on the facing page.

1. Admiral Fell Inn
888 South Broadway, Baltimore, MD 21231
www.admiralfell.com

If you want to stop by while you're in town, the inn contains two restaurants and a very nice pub. If you want to stay overnight, your visit comes with a ghost tour of the building and a chance to survey Fells Point from the rooftop observation deck. Beautifully restored, the building is well worth a visit, whether for a quick drink in the bar (keep an eye out for spectral nurses), dinner or lodging. Staff are usually happy to share their personal ghost stories with visitors!

2. Prohibition-era sign on building.
Shakespeare Street

The paint is fading because it's nearly one hundred years old; be sure to get a photograph while you're there!

3. Duda's Tavern
1600 Thames Street, Baltimore, MD 21231

A comfortable bar with a neighborhood feel, Duda's Tavern is located in one of the few triangular buildings in Fells Point. Operated by the Duda family since 1949, it is famous for its crab cakes and friendly vibe, as well as its resident spirit, the former merchant seaman and upstairs lodger affectionately known as "Doc." Listen for the sound of polka music from a long-gone jukebox.

4. Fell Family Cemetery
1607 Shakespeare Street

The original gravestones are long gone, but the two Edwards and both William Fells are commemorated on the current marker. A mysterious gentleman in sober colonial attire has been seen strolling to and from the cemetery, but opinions are divided as to which Fell he might be.

5. The Horse You Came In On Saloon
1626 Thames Street, Baltimore, MD 21231
www.thehorsebaltimore.com

Located in the heart of the harbor district, the Horse is a nice stop for an afternoon pint; it has loads of great interior wood and brickwork, a pressed-tin ceiling and some nice spooky spaces if you want to get away from the friendly noise at the bar. All sorts of phenomena have been reported on site, but listen for the sound of footsteps or the distant echo of Edgar Allan Poe ordering a final drink.

6. Fells Point Shipyards
Railway & Wharf

Now cleared of their crumbling warehouses, the waterfront where the shipbuilding yards once stood is now accessible to the public. Locust Point is visible across the Patapsco, as is much of waterfront Fells Point.

7. Rye Craft Cocktails (Formerly Leadbetters Tavern)
1639 Thames Street, Baltimore, MD 21231

With its brick walls and long, narrow bar, this is a classic waterfront tavern, and its location along the wharves meant that violence was no stranger within (or without) its walls. Ladies who venture alone to the restroom have been startled by the apparition of a desperate man, who appears to stand behind them in their mirrored reflection.

8. CAT'S EYE PUB
1730 Thames Street, Baltimore, MD 21231
www.catseyepub.com

The Cat's Eye offers live music every night of the week and boasts a nice beer selection but does not serve food. (There is no kitchen!) Stop by to listen to a variety of genres, from classic blues to alt-rock, and be sure to check out the "Wall of Death" and the brothel door that was once connected to the ground floor by a staircase. If you're in the building as darkness begins to fall, sit at the end of the bar closest to the windows and keep an ear open for the sound of clicking electrical switches.

MERCHANTS HOUSE AND THE HORSE TROLLEY BARN (THE FELLS POINT VISITOR CENTER)
1724–26 Thames Street
Open 10:00 a.m.–4:00 p.m. daily
www.preservationsociety.com

Two doors from the Cat's Eye, you'll find the visitor center. There have been several sightings of ghosts in the buildings, but chances are small that you'll notice them in the crowd! But it's a neat building, and you can get lots of information about historic Fells Point and the preservation efforts that are an ongoing affair. And who knows? The person you thought was a costumed tour guide might just surprise you and walk right through a wall.

9. ROBERT LONG HOUSE
The Society for the Preservation of Federal Hill and Fells Point
812 South Ann Street Historic Fells Point, Baltimore, MD 21231
www.preservationsociety.com/about-us/robert-long-house.html

Tours of the first floor, which was furnished as a bicentennial project by the Maryland State Society of the Daughters of the American Revolution, are available upon reservation. The second floor, which was restored after a fire in 1999, houses preservation society offices.

10. The Wharf Rat
801 South Ann Street, Baltimore, MD 21231
www.thewharfrat.com

Stop by this cozy bar on a cold night and enjoy the fire; it's also a great stop in the summer. The authors can vouch for the quality of the hospitality, as well as the fish and chips and beer selection, but be alert for the sound of running footsteps behind the bar or for watches or electronics to go a little bit haywire around 5:00 p.m.

11. Rye Fells Point
807 South Broadway, Baltimore, MD 21231
www.ryebaltimore.com

It's not hard to figure out what kind of liquor they specialize in at Rye, but they do offer other beverages, and the bar is definitely worth checking out, whether you see a ghost or not. But be alert for the apparition of a man mounting a staircase that no longer exists, and check photographs for any unfamiliar faces.

12. Max's Taphouse
737 South Broadway, Baltimore, MD 21231
www.maxs.com

According to one of the inscriptions on the ceiling beams at Max's, "Beer makes you feel the way you ought to feel without beer," and they have a lot of beer: 102 taps and more than 1,000 bottles! Stop by to check out the pressed-tin ceiling, wooden floors and the relaxed atmosphere, but keep an eye out for customers who seem to come out of the walls.

13. Bertha's Mussels
734 South Broadway, Baltimore, MD 21231
www.berthas.com

Bertha's is a Fells Point institution. The downstairs bar isn't huge, but the crowd is usually people moving to or from their tables, where they eat the mussels for which Bertha's is famous. You can see just about anybody at Bertha's, and that includes ghosts; the building is the site of multiple hauntings that have been extensively investigated. From paranormal patrons at the bar to terrifying apparitions on the top floor, this location is packed with those that (perhaps) did not possess the muscles to leave. Be sure to get an "Eat Bertha's Mussels" bumper sticker before you flee in terror.

14. STICKY RICE (formerly Friends Bar)
1634 Aliceanna Street
www.bmoresticky.com

While the site is now occupied by an Asian-fusion restaurant, it has lost none of its historic vibe—especially in the bar. Most of the paranormal activity in this building has occurred on the second floor, but it's entirely possible that the sound of squeaking bedsprings and erotic moans could be heard downstairs.

THE CAPTAIN'S HOTEL (not open to the public)
1629–31 Aliceanna Street, Baltimore, MD 21231

Almost directly across the street from Sticky Rice, you'll see a building covered in formstone, which is a type of building sheathing that Baltimore filmmaker John Waters once described as the "polyester of brick." Made popular in the mid-twentieth century because it offered a cheap way to cover and seal the crumbling brick faces of downtown row houses, formstone's distinctive faux "natural stone" is strongly associated with the image of Baltimore itself. But while they don't look very impressive, these two row houses contained one of the most famous brothels in Baltimore. Now owned by the preservation society, the buildings are closed to the general public pending renovation.

15. 713 SOUTH ANN (not open to the public)

This restored building, the home of Patrick Travis, a prominent sea captain, was built around 1800. The figure of a bearded man wearing a dark coat and blue breeches is frequently spotted in the back lot, which is visible from Durham Street. Be sure to wave at him if you see him—according to local legend, he'll answer your wave and then vanish!

Notes

Introduction

1. Excerpt translated by Julia Dray. Original Latin text from A.J. Church and W.J. Brodribb, eds., *Select Letters of Pliny the Younger* (London: Longmans, Green, 1871).

Chapter 1

2. Published in 1612, Smith's charts remained in use for nearly seventy years; an early version was stolen by the Spanish in 1609, known as the "Zuñiga map." Smith's journals provide a glimpse of a vanished landscape; here, he describes anchoring on the Middle Branch of the Patapsco River: "We passed many shallow creekes, but the first we found Navigable for a ship, we called Bolus, for that the clay in many places under the clifts by the high water marke, did grow up in red and white knots as gum out of trees; and in some places so participated together as though they were all of one nature, excepting the coulour, the rest of the earth on both sides being hard sandy gravell." His voyages around the Chesapeake showed Smith a world that was filled with natural resources: "Beares, Martins and minkes we found, and in divers places that aboundance of fish, lying so thicke with their heads above the water,

as for want of nets (our barge driving amongst them) we attempted to catch them with a frying pan: but we found it a bad instrument to catch fish with: neither better fish, more plenty, nor more variety for smal fish, had any of us ever seene in any place so swimming in the water, but they are not to be caught with frying pans."

3. De Sousa, who was of African Portuguese descent, was one of the nine indentured servants who accompanied Jesuit missionaries on the *Ark* in 1634. He completed his indenture in 1638 and began to trade in furs and captain his own small ship. De Sousa is recorded as a member of the 1642 assembly of freedmen in St. Mary's City, and he led several trading voyages and mastered a ketch for the provincial secretary, John Lewger. Sadly, De Sousa vanishes from the record in 1642, and his ultimate fate is unknown.

4. Tobacco is native to the Americas, and there is evidence of purposeful cultivation that goes back nearly three thousand years; Native Americans used it as a trade item and used its smoke in rites and ceremonies. The tobacco species used in modern cigarettes, *Nicotiana tabacum*, exists only in cultivation and represents hundreds of years of domestication; in the wild, there are more than seventy species.

5. The term *hooker* is said by some to have originated in the brothels of Fells Point; others point to Civil War general Joseph Hooker, whose divisions were accompanied by so many prostitutes that the ladies were known as "Hooker's Brigade." In his *Dictionary of Americanisms*, published in 1859, John Bartlett identifies the term as emanating from a New York neighborhood known as Corlear's Hook. The word itself dates back to at least 1567 and may originally have referred to men and women who would "hook" a purse out of one's pocket; another source claims that a "hooker" was a cheap but serviceable working boat used in the ports of Europe—not much to look at, but in fairly sound condition.

6. The *Chasseur* was the prototype for the modern *Pride of Baltimore I* and *II*.

7. Great Britain did not recognize the right of a British subject to relinquish his status as a subject of the Crown by immigrating to another country—once a British subject, always a British subject. Anyone born in the dominion was considered a citizen regardless of parental status. Children born to visitors or foreigners were considered citizens. Britain did not consider that citizenship could be acquired—a foreigner was always a foreigner (except by virtue of a special grant of citizenship). This rationale of natural-born citizenship presumes

the existence of a "natural allegiance" to the Crown as a "debt of gratitude." As this debt could never be repaid, citizenship by birth was perpetual and could not be removed or revoked. Great Britain was not alone in this insistence on a natural allegiance; many nations held to this philosophy of citizenship until late in the nineteenth century. Britain itself did not change its policy until 1870.

8. Opened in 1688 in London, Lloyd's Coffee House was an indispensable meeting place where merchants and ship owners conducted business. Reputable businessmen were allowed to rent a table from which to conduct business, and private rooms were available when secrecy was desired. The founder of the coffeehouse, Edward Lloyd (1658–1713), acted as a broker, held deposit money and escrow accounts and eventually expanded into insuring cargoes for owners and captains worthy of trust. The business profited and expanded, and today, Lloyd's of London is one of the largest corporations in the shipping industry, handling not only insurance but also everything to do with international commerce and shipping.

9. In 1827, an eight-year-old slave named Fred Bailey was sent to Fells Point by his master and apprenticed to a ship's caulker; he later wrote that "going to live at Baltimore laid the foundation, and opened the gateway, to all my subsequent prosperity." His new master, Hugh Auld, lived in a home at the corner of Aliceanna Street and Happy Alley (now Durham Street). With the aid of freedmen from his Baltimore church, Fred Bailey disguised himself as a sailor and escaped to the North, where he changed his name. Frederick Douglass never again lived in Fells Point, but the great abolitionist writer and orator felt a strong personal bond with the neighborhood.

10. The "Baltimore Mud Machine" was invented in 1785 by John and Andrew Ellicott, established flour exporters and owners of the largest grain mill on the East Coast (Ellicott Mills), whose export warehouses were located at Pratt and Light Streets. Initially powered by horses, the machine was later outfitted with a steam engine, and the Ellicott Machine Company (now Ellicott Dredges) has since helped build and maintain the Panama Canal, among other international projects. By the 1790s, the City of Baltimore had imposed a five-pound fine on anyone who deposited any dirt, construction debris or other materials that might wash into the basin.

CHAPTER 2

11. The mutiny on the HMS *Hermione* in 1797 offers a glimpse into what life at sea could be like under a sadistic captain. In February 1797, Captain Hugh Pigot was given command of HMS *Hermione* after serving a nine-month term as captain of the HMS *Success*, during which he ordered no fewer than eighty-five floggings (equivalent to half of the crew); the whippings caused at least two deaths. Aboard the *Hermione*, he instituted the practice of flogging whichever sailor was the last down to the deck. Dissatisfied with the crews' performance during a storm, he gave the order that the last men down to the deck would be flogged; in their panicked rush to the deck, three young sailors fell to their deaths, one of them landing on an officer, wounding him. Pigot ordered the crew to "throw the lubbers overboard," an insult that enraged the sailors; when they complained, a number of them were also flogged. The mutiny that exploded in late September 1797 resulted in the death of Pigot, who was hacked to pieces in his cabin, as were most of the ship's officers. Mr. Southcott, the ship's master, had been seriously injured by the falling sailor and was unable to defend himself, but he was spared by the mutineers, who needed him to guide the ship into Spanish waters. The Spanish took *Hermione* into their navy, but it was subsequently recaptured by the British in a daring raid and returned to service as the HMS *Retaliation*. The majority of the mutineers were captured and tried; most of them were executed or transported, although several of the younger crew members were pardoned, thanks to testimony from Mr. Southcott.
12. In 1841, the *Naval Journal of the American Seamen's Friend Society* described the benefit of the boardinghouse and its religious mission: "The cause of temperance is advancing among seamen in Baltimore, and a boardinghouse of good character has been established for their accommodation when on shore…and this house…has nevertheless been productive of considerable good, in partially counteracting the evils which have long existed in the ordinary sailor boarding-houses. Some of the landlords have thrown down their bars, and all deal out the liquid poison more secretly and cautiously than formerly."

CHAPTER 3

13. In the early years of American history, prostitutes demanded equal treatment under the law and sued individuals for damages, such as those that occurred in 1830s New York City. "Brothel riots," where civilians forcibly entered and vandalized prostitutes' homes and workplaces, were not uncommon, as neighborhoods sought to drive out a brothel. The target in the riots was not the prostitutes, but their property (bed, furniture and so on).

14. Running a brothel was an expensive proposition that came with significant risk; buying in wasn't cheap, and neither was opening a new establishment. There were a number of expenses—especially in the late nineteenth century, when bribes to police and civil authorities were necessary to remain in operation; commonly assessed as "fines," the money went to police, magistrates, elected officials and others and ensured that the authorities turned a blind eye to the brothel's activities. The yearly fee for a liquor license was between $75 to $300; the annual fine for a brothel with four working girls could total more than $1,200. Several Baltimore brothels paid in excess of $3,000 per year in "fines" during the nineteenth century.

15. Just to the east of Fells Point, in the Canton neighborhood, 2920 Elliott Street dates back to the 1880s. The building had a tavern on the first floor that was known as the "Blue Lantern," and the second and third floors contained a warren of nearly thirty rooms and a small door to the alley that gave access to a small room that contained a ladder to the second floor.

16. One locally infamous example of a man marrying a working girl involves the family who started the investment bank Alex Brown and Sons in Baltimore in the early 1800s; a scion of the family, Alexander Brown, died in 1892, and his unusual obituary told the story: "Baltimore, March 20, 1892—Alexander Brown seventy-three years died here to-day. He was a member of the well-known family of bankers, but was outlawed from society on account of his marriage to Laura Hobson. This woman was the daughter of his father's lodge keeper. Brown fell in love with her and would have married her then, but she disappeared, and when next he met her she was the leader of the local demi-monde [high-class prostitute]. He persuaded her to marry him, and the result was the greatest scandal in the history of Baltimore Society. He took his bride to his magnificent country place, Brooklyn Wood, in the midst of the most aristocratic neighborhood of the State, and there, with convivial spirits, big celebrations and orgies

were held. The match resulted in cross-suits for divorce. Mr. Brown won the case, but the woman Hobson got $3,000 a year and kept her dower rights. Those rights will now yield her from one to two hundred thousand dollars. Mr. Brown was accomplished, but, unlike his family, which represents much of what is best in the life of the city, he had no taste for business, and his gay career made for him a very miserable old age." *New York Times*, March 21, 1892.

17. "Short after 6 o'clock this evening Capt. Thomas C. Hance, commander of an oyster schooner, shot and killed his wife, Annie E. Hance, in a brothel on Spring Street, near Baltimore. The ball penetrated her skull just behind the right ear and passed into the brain, causing almost instant death. As soon as the shooting was done Hance left the house and went to his vessel on the south side of the basin, where he was soon after arrested. He states that he met his wife in the house where she was killed more than two years ago and induced her to leave it after which he married her. They went to housekeeping and lived happily together until last April, when he left home to prosecute his business. When he returned he found his home deserted, and after a search discovered that his wife had returned to the place where he first met her. He tried to induce her to go with him to their home, but did not succeed. When he again went away he wrote to her, addressing her as 'my dear wife,' and begged her to return to his care and affections, but she remained obdurate. This evening, when there were only three persons in the house, he gained access through the rear and went immediately to her room on the upper floor. He again begged her to go with him, but she persistently refused, when he shot her and then placed the revolver in a drawer of a stand in the room. She was known in the house as Kate Le Roy, and in that name he addressed letters to her when he was absent from the city. Mrs. Hance was but twenty-two years old." *Baltimore Sun*, September 28, 1885. (The trial of Thomas Hance concluded in November 1885, and he was found not guilty by reason of insanity.)

CHAPTER 4

18. In 1777, George Washington ordered mandatory inoculation for troops if they had not survived a smallpox infection earlier in life. Benedict Arnold's troops had failed to capture Quebec from Britain the year before because more than half of the colonial troops had smallpox.

19. When the Philadelphia epidemic ended in November 1793, the death toll stood at more than 5,000, nearly 1 of every 6 residents. In four months, the disease wiped out entire families, wreaking economic and social havoc on a scale never before seen in the new nation. By comparison, 4,435 Americans died in battle over the eight years of the Revolutionary War.

20. "The first case of yellow fever, that I saw, was on the 7th of August. The patient was in the fourth day of the disease, and had been harassed several hours with the vomiting of that dark fluid, so greatly resembling strong coffee muddy with its grounds. His eyes had been very red, but were now, together with his skin, yellow: the latter was dry and cool; his pulse was slow and full. He was either oppressed with stupor—or deranged with a mild delirium. In a few hours he was dead. I could not pause a moment in believing his disease to be the yellow fever. I mentioned freely what I had seen, and expressed my apprehensions that this case might prove the prelude of a scene of calamity. The Point was now becoming considerably sickly, and many deaths occurred there suddenly, or after a very short indisposition." Account of the yellow fever in Baltimore, in 1793, by Dr. Thomas Drysdale, in a letter to Dr. Benjamin Rush, 1795.

21. The documents or articles that mention this "mass grave" are devoid of links to historical documents or articles; in fact, many of these documents reference one another as proof. As best can be determined, once upon a time, somebody once told a story about an illegal yellow fever burial in Fells Point, and the story just exploded from there. It is exceedingly unlikely that valuable land in the very center of town would be used for burials, especially as the Broadway Market was a growing concern and is located next to the purported location of the "mass grave." The land around the Fells Point harbor was very wet; flooding was common along Broadway. No one with any sense was going to dig a deep pit at that spot and fill it with rotting bodies. Even if the local inhabitants didn't understand the sanitary issues, the stench alone would have been enough to keep them from doing it.

Chapter 5

22. When a mob in Baltimore pursued a federal agent and blocked in his truck, knocking him unconscious and making off with one hundred cases of beer that had just been confiscated, Maryland governor Richie dryly observed that the gentleman in charge of the federal "dry officers" should

"take measures for the better safeguarding of prohibition officers in the discharge of their duties." No one was ever prosecuted.

CHAPTER 6

23. More than three-quarters of the tea consumed in the colonies was illegal; in 1756–57, more than four hundred chests of tea were imported into Philadelphia, but only sixteen entered legally. British government estimates in 1763 calculated that smuggled commodities accounted for nearly £700,000 per year, an enormous sum at that time.

24. This conflict is usually referred to as the French and Indian War in the United States, but Native Americans fought for both Great Britain and France. The North American conflict was a small part of what is called the Seven Years' War.

25. Americans were not the only people who liked inexpensive tea—over half the tea in England entered illegally. Like their American counterparts, English smugglers found the customs restrictions to be an infringement on trade rights and were often indignant when their ships and cargoes were seized. And we just had to include the following letter because it's the best letter of complaint we've seen in a long time. It was sent by the owner of a seized vessel (who was not on board at the time) to Captain Bursack of the *Speedwell*, a British revenue cutter: "Sir: Damn thee and God damn thy two purblind eyes thou bugger, thou death-looking son of a bitch. O, that I had been there (with my company) for thy sake when thou tookest them men of mine on board the Speedwell cutter on Monday, the 14th of December. I would drove thee and thy gang to Hell where thou belongest, thou Devil incarnet. Go down, thou Hell Hound, unto thy kennel below and bathe thyself in that sulphurous lake that has been so long prepared for such as thee, for it is time the world was rid of such a monster. Thou art no man but a devil, thou fiend. O Lucifer, I hope thou will soon fall into Hell like a star from the sky, there to lie unpitied and unrelented of any for ever and ever, which God grant of his infinite mercy. Amen."

26. An American merchant, writing to a friend in Amsterdam, said in 1748, "The sweets of the French trade by way of flags of truce has put me upon turning my navigation that way, which is the most profitable business I know of. But, my friend, of this you must not lisp a word."

27. *Baltimore Sun* archive.

Chapter 7

28. Michael Carter, personal account.

Chapter 8

29. The alleys, which existed to allow access to the back lots of properties fronting on the major streets and were lined with inexpensive housing for laborers, were later designated as through streets, and many of the names were changed in 1822. Some simply became "Street" instead of "Alley" (like Madeira, Castle and Spring), while others were completely renamed: Strawberry Alley became Dallas Street, Apple became Bethel, Star became Chapel and the wonderfully named Happy Alley became drab old Durham Street.

Chapter 9

30. The Robert Long House was constructed with a "pent roof," which extends across the façade, unique for Maryland homes of this era, and incorporated glazed header bricks. The symmetry of the masonry is partially a result of well-laid bricks and partially an optical illusion: the deep vine joint carved into the mortar tricks the eye into ignoring the mismatched sizes of the bricks.

31. Many supporters of English rule were forced to flee to Canada or Great Britain to escape violence at the hands of rebellious colonists, leaving behind substantial properties and estates. Following the American Revolution, many exiles petitioned Congress and the various state legislatures for remuneration, most often to no avail. Many early American fortunes were created in this appropriation of assets.

32. James Biays (1760–1822) was a successful shipbuilder and entrepreneur. After losing several ships to the British naval blockade of European ports (the Royal Navy seized not only his ships and cargoes but also any sailor deemed a British deserter), James Biays became a firm supporter of declaring war against Great Britain. In the summer of 1812, he was accused of fomenting a mob that destroyed the printing press of a newspaper opposing the conflict, and during the Battle of North Point, Biays commanded one of the cavalry units that drove the British back

to their ships. Both he and his brother Joseph helped with building the hasty fortifications that protected Baltimore Harbor. In the years after the war, his business interest expanded, his wharves on Thames Street were extended and he and his brother received a monopoly on providing fresh water to Fells Point—along with the responsibility of paying for all the upkeep. Both Joseph and James were active in Baltimore politics; by 1820, James Biays no longer called himself a shipbuilder but a merchant.

CHAPTER 11

33. Originally called a private man-o-war, ships operating under such a commission became known as "privateers," a name that extended to the captain and crew; in France, the commissions were called "lettres de course," which sailor vernacular shortened to "corsairs."
34. During the War of 1812, the American privateer *General Armstrong* is credited with delaying the British fleet's arrival in Louisiana long enough to allow Andrew Jackson to get into position to inflict a humiliating defeat on the Royal Navy at the Battle of New Orleans in 1815. Attacked by three British warships in the neutral harbor of Fayal, in the Azores, the *Armstrong* seriously damaged two and inflicted heavy casualties on the crews of all three vessels before the privateer crew scuttled their vessel and escaped to the shore.
35. During the American Revolution, the colonial legislatures and the Continental Congress granted at least 1,700 letters of marque and commissioned nearly eight hundred vessels as privateers, which were later credited with capturing or destroying about six hundred British ships. The estimated damage to British shipping was close to $18 million (approximately $450 million in 2012 dollars), and that prize money did much to repair the economy of the new United States; many of the wealthiest families of New England got their founding capital from privateering.
36. The British navy was a harsh service, and British sailors were known to desert at any opportunity. Because American shipping was neutral at the start of the conflict, many a British sailor jumped ship and made his way onto a vessel flying the U.S. flag. British warships began to stop and search American shipping, seizing any sailors they thought might be deserters. Britain did not recognize the right of a British subject to relinquish his status as a subject of the Crown or immigrate and transfer his national

allegiance as a naturalized citizen to any other country. The United States recognized British-born sailors on American ships as Americans; Britain did not and impressed not only British-born sailors but also any suspicious passenger. Outrage over this challenge to American sovereignty was a driving force behind the eventual declaration of war.

37. During the War of 1812, American forces tried numerous times to break through English lines in lower Canada in order to advance on Montreal. In February 1814, Major General James Wilkinson set out with 4,000 men and eleven pieces of artillery; American troops attempted to cross a bridge over the strongly flowing Lacolle River, only to encounter a British garrison unit centered around Lacolle Mill. The garrison under the command of Major Richard Handcock was small: 180 British soldiers and Marines and 160 Canadian Fencibles (an infantry unit), but Wilkinson could only fire three of his cannons and his attempted bombardment of the mill was ineffective. The British troops, however, were running out of ammunition, and the commander decided to attempt to capture the American artillery although he was outnumbered nearly 12 to 1. Handcock's first assault failed, but British reinforcements arrived and he attempted a second, which succeeded in a brief seizure of the artillery until American troops forced them to retreat. As the darkness of a winter night closed in, Wilkinson retreated, with at least 254 men killed or wounded in comparison to British losses of 61 men.

38. The text of Boyle's proclamation included the following: "I do, therefore, by virtue of the power and authority in me vested (possessing sufficient force), declare all the ports, harbors, bays, creeks, rivers, inlets, outlets, islands and sea coast of the United Kingdom of Great Britain and Ireland in a state of strict and rigorous blockade….And I do hereby caution and forbid the ships and vessels of all and every nation in amity and peace with the United States, from entering or attempting to enter, or from coming or attempting to come out of any of the said ports, harbors, bays, creeks, rivers, inlets, outlets, islands or sea coast under any pretence whatsoever!"

39. Soon after the War of 1812 began, Captain Boyle took command of the privateer *Comet* and on his first cruise captured four vessels worth nearly $400,000. On the second voyage, he sailed the Brazilian coast and made five captures; unfortunately, British cruisers retook all five. On his next voyage, in October 1813, he and his ship cruised to the West Indies and captured twenty prizes before returning in March 1814. Boyle left *Comet* and took command of the privateer *Chasseur*, of which he was part owner. Boyle set his course for the British Isles via the Grand Banks and sailed

along the coasts of Britain and Ireland, acquiring eighteen prize ships before returning to New York on October 24.

40. The British intended a two-pronged assault: five thousand soldiers under Major General Robert Ross were to be landed on North Point and move south and west to attack the city from the undefended northeast, while naval vessels began a bombardment of Fort McHenry and the harbor fortifications. Once they had breached the harbor defenses, marines would be landed in the city center with the sole mission of firing the city and destroying the shipyards. The British land attack managed to break through at several points, but General Ross fell to a sniper's bullet on the first day. His successor was a cautious man who found the internal defenses far stronger than anticipated; unwilling to press an attack, he ordered British forces to retreat to the ships on the afternoon of September 13. The naval assault also proved a failure; the marines who landed were unable to penetrate the fortifications and were forced to return to the ships. The British captains decided to attack the fort from the safety of their fleet. On the evening of September 13, 1814, in the midst of a horrific thunderstorm, nineteen massed British vessels commenced a bombardment that rivaled the thunder.

41. Two of the most famous privateer captains from Baltimore were Thomas Boyle, who had commanded the vessels *Comet* and *Chasseur* during the war, and John Daniel Danels. During the Spanish-American War, Boyle did not repeat his spectacular captures, but Danels became one of the heroes of the struggle for Venezuelan independence. From 1820 to 1824, Danels was part of Simón Bolívar's navy, blockading the coasts of Venezuela and Colombia against Spanish shipping. Danels's contribution to the revolution was later honored with a statue on the grounds of the Venezuelan Naval Academy.

42. The Confederacy *did* issue letters of marque and privateering commissions early in the Civil War, but the profits realized were too small for captains to persist, and most turned to running arms or other cargoes through Union blockades of Southern ports.

43. In one of the earliest recorded pirate tales, the Roman general and consul Gaius Julius Caesar was captured by a band of Cilician pirates when he was twenty-five years old. The pirate leader, Polygonus, set his ransom at the standard rate for a Roman nobleman, but Caesar ordered him to double the demand, after informing the pirate chief that he was not a "standard" Roman nobleman. Caesar's slave, Burgundus, was dispatched to arrange the ransom with the nearest Roman authorities, while the future emperor

remained at the pirate stronghold. During a stay that lasted several weeks, the Roman charmed his captors with his wit, often joking with them about his intentions to come back and destroy their stronghold once he had been released. Although the pirates were confident that he would never find his way back to their well-hidden fortress, Caesar returned with a fleet, destroyed the settlement and crucified every pirate, paying special attention to Polygonus.

44. One of Kidd's sailors, Theophilus Turner, parted ways with the captain in Philadelphia before his surrender and made his way south along the Chesapeake Bay, ready to use his share of the treasure for a comfortable retirement in the Tidewater. While at anchor in the Severn River, his ship was boarded by Maryland officials. Turner was arrested, his booty confiscated, and he was sent to England for trial; found guilty, he was pardoned just prior to his hanging.

45. There are a number of stories that a portion of Kidd's missing treasure lies buried somewhere near Maryland's Gibson Island, which lies just to the south of Baltimore. Others place it on Oak Island, Ocracoke Island, Cape May, Gardiners Island and the coast of the Bay of Fundy—locations all up and down the North American coast. No sign of buried treasure has been found at any of these locations, but many people continue to look. One man, Michael Smith, claimed to have found evidence of Kidd's treasure on an isolated Vietnamese island; after being arrested by Vietnamese authorities, he was jailed and later forced to leave the country.

Sources

Interviews

We would like to thank the employees, customers and owners of the following
locations for sharing their stories with us:

Admiral Fell Inn
Baltimore City Police Department
Bertha's Mussels
Cat's Eye Pub
The Horse You Came In On Saloon
Maryland Historical Society
The Preservation Society of Fells Point
The Robert Long House
The Wharf Rat

Books

Andreas, Peter. *Smuggler Nation: How Illicit Trade Made America*. New York:
Oxford University Press, 2013.

Behr, Edward. *Prohibition: Thirteen Years that Changed America*. New York: Arcade
Publishing, 1996.

Chapelle, Suzanne Ellery Greene. *Baltimore: An Illustrated History*. Woodland Hills, CA: Windsor Publications, 1980.

Lee, Robert Earl. *Blackbeard the Pirate: A Reappraisal of His Life and Times*. Winston-Salem, NC: John F. Blair Publishing, 1974.

Little, Benerson. *Pirate Hunting: The Fight against Pirates, Privateers, and Sea Raiders from Antiquity to the Present*. Dulles, VA: Potomac Books, 2010.

Luskey, Brian P., and Wendy A. Woloson. *Capitalism by Gaslight: Illuminating the Economy of Nineteenth-Century America*. Philadelphia: University of Pennsylvania Press, 2015.

Owens, Hamilton. *Baltimore on the Chesapeake*. Garden City, NY: Doubleday, Doran & Company, 1941.

Ringdal, Nils Johan. *Love for Sale: A World History of Prostitution*. New York: Grove Press, 2004.

Rukert, Norman G. *The Fells Point Story*. Baltimore, MD: Bodine & Associates, 1976.

Stern, Ellen Norman, *The French Physician's Boy: A Story of Philadelphia's 1793 Yellow Fever Epidemic*. Philadelphia, PA: XLibris, 2000.

Stockett, Maria Letitia. *Baltimore: A Not Too Serious History*. Baltimore, MD: Norman Remington Company, 1928.

Print Sources

The Anchorage Eighteenth Annual Report. Baltimore, MD: The Anchorage, 1909.

Baltimore Sun. "Statistics of the Slums: Result of an Official Investigation in Baltimore and Other Cities." July 28, 1894.

Fifth Annual Report of the Port Mission of Baltimore City. Baltimore, MD: Fleet, McGinley & Company, 1889.

SOURCES

Ordinances of the Mayor and City Council of Baltimore. Baltimore, MD: George W. Bowen & Company, 1858.

NEWSPAPERS AND ARCHIVES

Baltimore City Archives
Baltimore Sun
Capital-Gazette
Fells Point Preservation Society
Historic American Buildings Survey, National Park Service Database
Maryland Historical Society
New York Public Library Photo Archive
Washington Post

ABOUT THE AUTHORS

Mike Carter began his ghost tour in 2002 after six months of extensive research into the history and hauntings of Annapolis. He is a successful entrepreneur and marketing consultant who has been part of numerous technology start-ups and has consulted with the City of Annapolis on various projects pertaining to tourism in the historic city. Mike attended the University of Maryland at College Park, where he earned a bachelor's degree in English while also working out of the Dingman Center for Entrepreneurship, which incubated his love for business. When weekends came around, he could often be found in historic 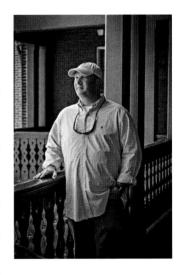 Annapolis, walking the streets and visiting the city's many haunted pubs. His popular and highly regarded Annapolis Ghost Tour is consistently rated in the top five paranormal tours in the country, while his Baltimore tours are quickly becoming just as popular and well received and can be found at www.toursandcrawls.com. He lives in Annapolis with his wife and young son, and when he isn't out stalking ghosts or interesting historical tidbits, he can be found out on the Chesapeake Bay sailing competitively or buzzing around on the family's powerboat.

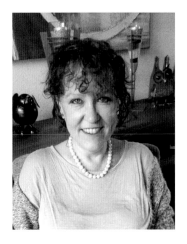

JULIA DRAY is a professional musician, writer and performer who lived in Annapolis for more than thirty years. After attending St. John's College, she worked as a restaurant manager, technical writer, magazine editor and pianist before joining Annapolis Ghost Tours in 2007; locals and visitors alike know her as the "ghost tour lady." After the publication of her first book, *Haunted Annapolis: Ghosts of the Capital City*, she retired from leading tours to focus on historical writing as well as musical composition and performance. She currently lives just outside Amsterdam, with her partner, Rob, two cats and many untidy stacks of books.

Visit us at
www.historypress.net
....
This title is also available as an e-book